OBAMA
WHY **BLACK**
AMERICA

SHOULD
HAVE
DOUBTS

To Barbara
Be Strong!
Be Free!

WILLIAM OWENS, JR.

Obama: Why Black America Should Have Doubts
Copyright © 2008 by William Owens
willpublish@gmail.com

Published by:
iTouch Publishers
www.itouchpublishers.com

Owens, William, 1964
Obama: Why Black America Should Have Doubts
p. cm.
ISBN: 978-1-60702-073-8

1. Owens, William 1964 2. Clergy
1st Printing 2008

All Scripture quotations are taken from the Holy Bible King James
Version

Cover Design Concept: W. Owens
Picture by Erik Kabik Photography

Printed in the United States of America

Contents

ACKNOWLEDGEMENTS

Any effort that is designed to challenge the status quo will always be in need of the support of people. This work is a prime example of this and would not be possible without a team effort of individuals that I am most appreciative of.

Above all to God, for His impartation to me of grace, courage and boldness to speak to the critical issues that will affect our nation. There is a war before us and I consider these people my fellow soldiers.

To my wife, Selena, in handling the very detailed aspects and overall feedback of the manuscript. She also was a wonderful sounding board throughout the process.

To my children, Tiffany, Bethany and David for their candid discussion of issues that reflect many of their peers.

To my father, Bill Owens, for his encouragement towards me to speak my convictions.

To Alveda King for her belief in the project and championing this message from day one.

To Jim Sloan for his wonderful ability to grab the essence of my heart and smooth out the rough edges while bringing my thoughts into focus.

To Dana Erbrecht who was tremendous in arranging this manuscript to ensure that its delivery was on point.

To Tricia Erickson for circulating this message throughout the media world.

Thanks to Nina May, Dean Nelson, and Tim Johnson for their support, knowledge and advice.

Without business alliances, you simply cannot get to market no matter how important your message. A special thanks to NBN Books for taking on this project way past the eleventh hour to ensure distribution. I truly appreciate your support of this project and the invaluable feedback that improved it.

"Have I therefore become your enemy because I tell you the truth?"

Galatians 4:16

FOREWORD

For those who are offended by the subject matter in this book, please be reminded that America is still a "free" country. You can read the book, or you can choose not to. If you desire revelation, read on. If not, close the book now. The "choice" is yours.

William Owens, Jr. is a wonderfully married, family man. His research and appeal to readers go beyond popular sentiment. His approach to seek answers is compelling and refreshing, but he is not alone. A growing community of young Americans, red and yellow, Black and White, is seeking truth in a troubled time. This book is not about skin color. We are all one human race, and we cannot allow skin color to become a deal breaker in what once was a community of faith, united for life and family.

The excitement of having a man on the presidential ballot whose skin is browner than any in recent American history is something to consider. Many Black Americans are convinced that justice for those of us once known as "Negroes" in America will be done by electing a brown-skinned, African-European as President.

Obviously, America is hungry for change, but America is looking in the wrong place. Barack cannot deliver America. The Senator's politics are neither a blessing nor praiseworthy.

Senator Obama's answer to the ills of society, of higher government spending, weaker national defense, continued tax dollars to

Planned Parenthood, and support of gay marriage, are diametrically opposed to everything African Americans truly believe and an anathema to the dream of Dr. Martin Luther King, Jr.

Life is sacred. The Negro cannot win if he is willing to sacrifice the future of his children for immediate personal comfort and satisfaction. Every time Barack Obama supports abortion on demand, gay civil unions, and higher government spending, he is sacrificing the lives of our children, and releasing injustice into the heads and hearts of America.

There is no justice in the onslaught of oppressive anti-life measures, such as the racist practice of abortion on demand; anti-procreation legislation; unbalanced judicial tyranny leading to excess incarceration of our young; anti-choice in the education of our youth; and a negative graphic media leading to poverty of mind and spirit.

Real change means an end, not only to the war across the sea, but an end to the war in our streets here in America; an end to the war against our children's minds; an end to the racist war on the womb and an end to the attacks against procreative marriage.

The Good Book tells us this: Do what is just and right. Rescue from the hand of his oppressor the one who has been robbed. Do no wrong or violence to the alien, the fatherless or the widow, and do not shed innocent blood in this place.

Dr. Alveda King

Dr. Alveda C. King is the niece of Dr. Martin Luther King, Jr., Founder of King for America, Co-Founder of Black Americans for Real Change, and a Pastoral Associate with Priests for Life.

I f it were not for my wife and children's unwavering support and enthusiasm to take on this book project, I would not have done so. I recognize that I could be branded for the rest of my life for taking an unpopular stand against the first Black American to run for President of the United States. Nevertheless, I willingly accept the mantle that has fallen on me, and I am at peace with my decision because I firmly believe I must speak out.

Before the expected phalanx of critics attack me, let me spare everyone the trouble of trying to figure out my reasons for writing this important book. First, I am by no means experienced in the arena of politics. I went to high school and acquired one year of college. Afterwards, I served in the United States Air Force from which I received an honorable discharge.

I have been married to one woman, my dear Selena, for twenty-three years this October. We have four children, three of whom still reside at home with us. I am currently an entrepreneur and an unashamed preacher of the Gospel of Jesus Christ. I am proud to assert our family loves God. We love our country, and we are not afraid to fight for it by standing up and giving an account of our ideas, which we believe are in harmony with the very ideas that shaped this country and the Constitution of the United States of America!

If you are a Black American, I can only imagine how you feel if you take the title of this book at face value. Please do not make this mistake. This book is intended as a challenge to YOU. *Do not look at things as they appear, but see them as they really are.* Jesus said," *Do not judge according to appearance, but judge with righteous judgment."(John 7:24)* As for the complainers and naysayers, I simply ask that you turn your energy toward solutions rather than divisive bickering. No matter what your concern, be it White America or Black America, I am simply asserting my conviction that we exercise our right to get involved in the process of shaping this country and removing the mess instead of stirring it. If you refuse to support a genuine and constructive effort with your time, treasure, and voice to achieve real solutions to the complex problems that confront us, then I sincerely question your allegiance to the United States. On the other hand, if you are prepared to become a true patriot intent on protecting and preserving the freedoms you enjoy as a citizen of our wonderful country, then I challenge you to get involved at: www.blackarc.org

I'll say it unabashedly. I love my country. I have taught my children to love it as well. As an informed citizen, I can discuss with you our imperfections as a nation. We have our warts and our weaknesses. But the fact remains, America is unique; I believe we are exceptional. We are a powerful yet compassionate country that has been a great stabilizing force in the world. Indeed, America is a coveted land made up of resilient people from every tongue, tone, and temperament. It makes us who we are and despite our faults, —and we surely have them—we remain a country that I believe God has blessed and set forth as a beacon of hope and freedom for the entire world.

It is not my intent here to attack Barack Obama personally. Let that be emphatically understood. However, any discussion, in order to be meaningful, must draw attention to Barack Obama's character as well as his agenda and how both will impact the lives of Black Americans and our country as a whole.

My purpose is to challenge you to look deeper at Barack Obama. If you are honest, I think you will conclude—as have I and so many others—that Obama's agenda is both wicked from a Christian perspective and highly manipulative when it comes to Black Americans. Perhaps Obama knows this, or perhaps he does not realize what he is doing. I say this because powerful and influential advisors can easily manipulate inexperienced politicians. Newcomers to the national political arena like freshly-minted Senator Barack Obama can become deluded into thinking they are doing right when they are really doing wrong.

We must, as Black Americans, work hard and work smart to preserve what we have gained.

This leads me to the current presidential election and the reason for this book.

As a Black American, I have developed serious doubts about Senator Barack Obama. Based on what I have seen, read and heard, I have come to view him as potentially dangerous—for our country and in particular for Black Americans.

Obama's handsome features, physical stature, and attempt at eloquence combine to make him a charismatic politician. You must admit this can be a deadly combination for us as Black Americans. In my view, we tend to have an addiction to "feeling good." We are easily satisfied with goose bumps that go no deeper than our first layer of skin. We are often afraid to look deeper—beyond the obvious—because then we would have to be responsible for our choices and refute the belief that a person who looks like us will automatically "take care of us." It is the Black mindset that presses upon us to say, "Give the brother a chance."

On one level I confess I understand this tendency, yet we as Black Americans must move beyond this. Would you let someone you did not know enter your family circle to date your daughter in order to "give him a chance?" I doubt you would. Therefore, does it make sense to vote for Barack Obama for the same reason? Do you really want to vote someone into the highest office in the land just to "give the brother a chance?"

The purpose of this book is to challenge you as a Black American to look deeper at Barack Obama the man, his voting record, and his position on the important issues facing our country, which, unfortunately, seem to change with the next newscast.

I believe when you take time to look closely and dispassionately—and if you are truly honest with yourself—you will see a politician who is charismatic but seriously devoid of the kind of experience that qualifies him to be President of the United States. I think you will see a young man who is anything but candid about who he is, what he really believes, and who his associates are. Under real scrutiny Barack Obama emerges as a continuously morphing, media-made cyborg candidate. One is left asking, "Who or what is behind the Barack Obama phenomenon?" I'm not alone in this assessment. I cannot tell you how many discussions I have had with both prominent and ordinary Black Americans who have expressed serious doubts about Barack Obama and where he will take us as a society and as a nation.

I urge you, don't put your race before your principles, before the truth, before your family, and before your own country.

As human beings our principles are the sum total of what we are when no one is watching and what we really believe when we have our eyes closed and are listening to that still small voice within. I choose to believe this is God's presence in our lives helping us to seek and ultimately find wisdom. Think hard and look within as you take the measure of Barack Obama. When a candidate for the presidency of the United States wants to seriously weaken his country in a time of war with fanatical enemies; when a candidate wants to legalize homosexual marriage and damage our vital family structure; when a candidate seeks to implement drastic socialistic economic policies that will undercut our free-market economy; I say we, as a nation of FREE families, need to carefully consider just who this person is—Black or not!

Through the writing of this book, my family and I are attempting to speak directly to Black American families. However, let it also be a clarion call to all Americans. I ask that you carefully and prayerfully weigh my perceptions as well as the facts as they are laid before you in this book. When you look deep into your heart, I believe you will agree with me that we must defeat Senator Barack Obama in his quest to become President of this powerful country and its special people.

Raising the Standard,

William Owens

CHAPTER ONE

Exactly What Does
Barack Obama Believe?

As Black Americans, we find ourselves at a pivotal moment in our history. The excitement is palpable, the significance immense. As I write this, Barack Obama is poised to become the first Black American candidate to be nominated for President of the United States by one of our two major political parties. This is being hailed as a triumphal moment for Black Americans and for America itself. Historic for Black America, yes. Beneficent, unequivocally, no.

The Obama candidacy is nothing more than a media feeding frenzy built on hype, hysteria and intimidation. Hype because Obama really offers nothing concrete with his "hope" and "change" campaign rhetoric; hysteria because people have bought into the well-oiled media spin; and, intimidation because many people are afraid to scrutinize Obama and speak out because of the race issue. Barack Obama not only knows this, he *relies* on the hype, hysteria and intimidation, not to benefit America, but his own political aspirations.

If there were ever a time when it would be easy to say "give the brother a chance" this would surely be it. Yet in my heart of hearts, I refuse to do this. I will not remain silent out of fear of repercussions because it is politically incorrect for Blacks to challenge Blacks. In a post 9/11 world, too much is riding on the outcome of this election. An Obama presidency will not only change our country in fundamental ways that will damage our society and weaken our national security, it *will set back Black America.* When we blindly embrace a charismatic candidate, failing to give him the scrutiny we place on any other candidates, we are abdicating our responsibilities to the nation as a whole. It is high time for Black America, White America and all America to stop making their ethnicity such a big deal that we become zealous for our color over being zealous for what is right and what is truth.

As the Barack Obama phenomenon continues to unfold, ask yourself:

(1) Is Barack Obama really a Black American? Does he speak with the authentic voice of a Black American?

(2) What do we really know about Barack Obama and his agenda? Do his words, his voting record, and his choice of associates, have our country's best interest at heart? Will he do the right thing for Black America?

(3) Do Obama's positions on issues reflect or oppose those of the Black Christian community?

Let's take them one at a time.

Is Barack Obama Really A Black American?

When I look past the impressive salesmanship of Barack Obama, I see a person who does not resonate with our struggle as a people. Although I know I am not alone in this opinion, it is unfortunate few of us Black Americans are willing to step forward and say this publicly. So here it is. *Barack Obama does not and cannot relate to our past as Black Americans because in reality he is not a Black American.* I am continually dismayed that he insists on portraying himself as being so, and even more deeply troubled that the media, rather than responsibly reporting the facts, helps sustain this perception.

One thing you can say for sure about us as Black Americans — *we are Black and we are proud of it.* Now consider Barack Obama, who consistently touts his African roots. His heritage is Muslim—*not* African American. Ask yourself, "Why is Barack Obama not honest about his origin and, more importantly, why is he not proud of it? Why is he leading us to believe he is someone other than who he really is?" Because of our pride in our heritage, one's origin should be an acid test for us as Black Americans. If you cannot be honest and forthright about something this basic, how can you be trusted to be the leader of the free world?

Obama is not a Black American. With permission, below is an excerpt from an article written by columnist and author, Andy Martin. His book, *Obama: The Man Behind the Mask* is currently in bookstores.

"Obama's life story is vastly different from the one he portrays. My point: if he will lie about his mother and father, what else is he lying about?"

Fiction: Obama stated in his Convention speech: 'my father... grew up herding goats.' The 'goat herder' claim has been repeated endlessly. It is a lie.

Fact: Obama's grandfather, Hussein Onyango Obama was a prominent and wealthy farmer. His son, Obama's father, was a child of privilege, not privation. He was an outstanding student, not a herdsman.

Fiction: Obama was given an 'African' name.

Fact: Obama is a Muslim who has concealed his religion. Obama has a great opportunity to be forthright. Instead, he has treated his Muslim heritage as a dark secret. His grandfather was named 'Hussein.' That is an Arabic-Muslim, not African, name. Hussein was a devout Muslim and named his son, Barack Senior, 'Baracka.' Baracka is an Arabic word meaning 'blessed.' Baracka comes out of the Koran and Arabic, not Africa.

Barack Senior was also a devoted Muslim, and also chose a Muslim name for his son, our own Barack Obama, Junior. Again, his name was Arabic and Koranic.

Obama has spent a lifetime running from his family heritage and religious heritage. Would his father have given his son a Koranic name if the father were not a devout Muslim? Obama's stepfather was also a Muslim.

Fiction: Obama Senior was a harmless student 'immigrant' who came to the United States only to study.

Fact: Obama was part of one of the most corrupt and violent organizations in Africa: the Kenyatta regime. Obama's father ran back to Kenya soon after the British left. It is likely Obama's father had Mau Mau sympathies or connections, or he would not have been welcomed into the murderous inner circle of rapists, murderers, and arsonists. I believe Obama's secret shame at his family history of rape, murder and arson is what actualizes him. Our research is not yet complete. We are seeking to examine British colonial records. Our investigation to date has drawn on information on three continents.

> **Obama has spent a lifetime running from his family heritage and religious heritage**

And what about Obama's beloved Kenyan brothers and sisters? None of his family was invited to Boston to share his prominence. Are his relatives being kept in the closet? Where are they? More secrecy, more prevarication.

It is time for Barack Obama to stop presenting a fantasy to the American people. We are forgiving and many would still support him. It may well be that his concealment is meant to endanger Israel. His Muslim religion would obviously raise serious questions in many Jewish circles where Obama now enjoys support."

Barack Obama's birth certificate, which he has failed to provide the original to the public, has raised questions regarding his own American citizenship and the ability to become President under the Constitution.

The Israel Insider has run a six-part series on the birth certificate issue. The *Insider* cited a finding by a technical expert on the popular right-wing blog, *Atlas Shrugs*, which claims the certificate posted on Daily Kos, and later on Obama's own *Stop the Smears* site, is indeed a fake.

"The latest examination of the purported documents is by far the most detailed and technically sophisticated to date."

Atlas Shrugs publisher Pamela Geller reports that the expert analyst, who goes by the screen name "Techdude", is 'an active member of the Association of Certified Fraud Examiners, American College of Forensic Examiners, The International Society of Forensic Computer Examiners, International Information Systems Forensics Association — the list goes on. He also a board certified as a forensic computer examiner, a certificated legal investigator, and a licensed private investigator. He has been performing computer-based forensic investigations since 1993.'"

http://web.israelinsider.com/Articles/Politics/12993.htm

Why is Obama refusing to provide the American public with the original copy of his birth certificate? Perhaps Obama has something to hide. According to the *Insider*:

"The purported birth certificate was published by the Daily Kos on June 12 in response to unconfirmed reports that Obama was not in fact born in the United States (Canada and Kenya were suggested as the possible locations of his actual birth). Since he would in that case not be a natural born US citizen (his mother was not present in the US sufficiently long as an adult to pass American citizenship on to him automatically), he would not be eligible to be president."

The Insider concludes, "the bottom line is this: If Obama can't prove he has a certified Hawaiian birth certificate, he's not a natural born American. If he's not a natural born American, he can't be president. That's the law of the land."

http://web.israelinsider.com/Articles/Politics/12944.htm

http://web.israelinsider.com/Articles/Politics/12993.htm

Why does Barack Obama not admit his true heritage and continue to portray himself as a Black American when in fact he is not? Given his Muslim heritage why does he presume to speak for Black Americans? I, for one, believe Barack Obama is incapable of truly understanding what is best for Black Americans because he is really not one of us. Despite the evidence, it is inconceivable to me why many Black Americans believe they must embrace Barack Obama as one of them.

As American citizens, it is not only our right, but also our duty to question the motives and intentions of anyone running for office in the United States of America, especially when it concerns the individual who will sit in the Oval Office for the next four years. Is it not incumbent upon us as informed citizens to question whom that person really is—Black or White?

Black Americans overwhelmingly support Barack Obama over his opponent by a huge margin. According to a recent Gallup poll, 91% of Black Americans intend to vote for Barack Obama in November. Is this our "give the brother a chance" mentality at work? Our blind devotion to one particular candidate or political party regardless of the facts warrants our attention. Simply handing over the keys to our future and our children's future to a man whose record does not remotely parallel the values, traditions and struggles of Black America, is irresponsible and downright dangerous.

Black Americans for Real Change (BARC) co-founded by myself and Dr. Alveda C. King shares my concern: "My uncle, Dr. Martin Luther King, Jr. said: 'Cowardice asks the question—is it safe? Expediency asks the question - is it politic? Vanity asks the question—is it popular? But conscience asks the question—is it right? And there comes a time when one must take a position that is neither safe, nor politic, nor popular; but one must take it because it is right. Our lives begin to end the day we become silent about things that matter.' This is not the time to be silent; this is not the time to give Barack Obama a free pass! There is too much at stake."

When I look at Barack Obama, I see a crafty politician who is deceiving the general public by using a Black American persona in order to garner votes from the Black community. He cleverly points out that it has been forty years since Martin Luther King, Jr. made his famous "I Have a Dream" speech in Washington, DC, as though he somehow has a legitimate connection with our struggle and our victory. I am deeply disturbed by this.

My colleagues in BARC believe it is time for a wake up call to all Black Americans to take a closer look at the real Barack Obama. In our view, Obama's posturing is dishonest and, if successful, will harm the Black community and cripple our future potential for electing an authentic Black American to the presidency. As important as our heritage is to us, we should ensure it is entrusted to an honest and authentic Black American, rather than a pretender and panderer.

As Black Americans, we understand pain and perseverance. We are a forgiving people. In fact, one could say we forgive to a fault. But *don't make us out to be your fool*— and I'm afraid that's exactly what Barack Obama is doing, with the help of a well crafted media effort that glosses over the details of a side of him that would give us serious cause for doubt. And unfortunately, as Black Americans we seem to be buying into it.

Can this really be good for any of us—Black or White?

I do not think so. To me life, liberty and the pursuit of happiness means you are free to pursue *your* goals... *your* dreams. To fail. To succeed. To be self-reliant. I am one who does not wish to subjugate my liberty by giving power to politicians in the expectation they will act in my self-interest. *The agenda Barack Obama and his coterie of advisors have presented is wrong for us as Black Americans and bad for America.*

Barack Obama's Contradicts Most Black Americans

What do we really know of the Barack Obama agenda?

As things now stand, many Americans who support Barack Obama have trouble explaining what he stands for beyond vague concepts like "hope" and "change." As stated above, 91 percent of Black Americans intend to vote for Obama in November. According to a *New York Times* poll, 72 percent of Black Americans said that Barack Obama cares about them "a lot," and 83 percent of Black Americans have a favorable opinion of him. What does Black America really know about Barack Obama? The majority of Black Americans are against same-sex marriage and a legal recognition of same-sex civil unions, a yet only a meager five percent of Black Americans believe that abortion, moral or family issues were their main reason for supporting a presidential candidate, according to a Washington Post-ABC News poll. Why?

The following is a collection of quotes from speeches, interviews and press coverage of Barack Obama. Links to the original interviews and news sources are provided to ensure his remarks are not taken out of context. I urge you to delve deeply into these positions and reflect on their implications for us as Black Americans and for our country.

As you read the following information ask yourself how Obama's agenda reflects the will and wishes of the Black American family. Ask yourself, "what effect do these attitudes have for our families and the specific issues that face us? Does his attitudes reflect the majority of the Black American family's views?" Perhaps your opinions will change.

By a large margin, Black Americans widely oppose same-sex marriage. 67% of Black Americans favor the constitutional amendment that would define marriage between that of a man and a woman. A national survey by Pew Research Center in May shows only 26 percent of Blacks favor gay marriage, while 56 percent are opposed. According to a report by the National Black Justice Coalition and Freedom to Marry, approximately 75 percent of Black Americans believe homosexual relations are always wrong; and over one-third of Black Americans believe AIDS may a punishment for homosexual behavior.

> **75 percent of Black Americans believe homosexual relations are always wrong**

According to the report, on both of these issues, "overall, Blacks are 14 percentage points more likely to hold both positions than Whites."

While Obama falsely clings to a Black American heritage and cloaks himself in Christianity, his actions go directly against both. http://www.southernvoice.com/2008/7-18/news/national/8884.cfm (CBS news -67% AA oppose Constitutional amendment http://www.cbsnews.com/stories/2004/03/15/opinion/polls/main606453.shtml) (Southern Voice 2/3 of AA oppose Gay Marriage)

Barack Obama Believes Homosexuality is no More Immoral than Heterosexuality

"I don't think homosexuals are immoral any more than I think heterosexuals are immoral."

(Source: The Improbable Quest, by John K. Wilson, p.115 Oct 30, 2007)

Barack Obama Believes the Gay Rights Movement is Similar to the Civil Rights Movement

"My attitude is if people are being treated unfairly and unequally, then it needs to be fixed. So I'm always very cautious about getting into comparisons of victimology. You know, the issues that gays and lesbians face today are different from the issues that were faced by African-Americans under Jim Crow. That doesn't mean, though, that there aren't parallels in the sense that legal status is not equal. And that has to be fixed.

I'm going to be more sympathetic not because I'm Black. I'm going to be more sympathetic because this has been the cause of my life and will continue to be the cause of my life, making sure that everybody's treated fairly and that we've got an expansive view of America, where everybody's invited in and we are all working together to create the kind of America that we want for the next generation." (Source: 2007 HRC/LOGO debate on gay issues Aug 9, 2007) http://www.outfordemocracy.org/arch/000649.html

Barack Obama Opposes All State Marriage Amendments as "Divisive and Discriminatory."

Although Californians voted overwhelmingly to affirm traditional marriage in 2000, the California State Supreme Court struck down the ban in 2008. Californians responded by gathering over one million signatures to put an amendment to the state constitution on the ballot in November. Barack Obama wrote an open letter to the Alice B. Toklas Lesbian, Gay, Transgender and Bisexual Democratic Club in which he stated, "I oppose the divisive and discriminatory efforts to amend the California Constitution, and similar efforts to amend the U.S. Constitution or those of other states."

http://www.advocate.com/news_detail_ektid56867.asp

Barack Obama Intends to Fully Repeal the Defense of Marriage Act (DOMA)

The Defense of Marriage Act was signed into law by President Bill Clinton in 1996 in response to the redefinition of marriage to include same sex couples in Hawaii. DOMA allows states to refuse to recognize a gay marriage performed in another state. Obama reiterated his position in an interview with *The Advocate* that he would fully repeal DOMA. This means that a gay couple married in Massachusetts could then move to Georgia, and Georgia would be forced to recognize their marriage. http://www.advocate.com/exclusive_detail_id53285_Page3.asp

"Well, my view is that we should try to disentangle what has historically been the issue of the word "marriage," which has religious connotations to some people. But my job as president is going to be to make sure that the legal rights that have consequences on a day-to-day basis for loving same sex couples all across the country, that those rights are recognized and enforced by **my** White House and by **my** Justice Department." (Source: 2007 HRC/LOGO debate on gay issues Aug 9, 2007) http://www.outfordemocracy.org/arch/000649.html [emphasis mine]

Barack Obama Would Sign a Transgender-inclusive ENDA and Hate Crimes Legislation that Elevates Sexual Behavior to the Level of Race

The Employment Non-discrimination Act (ENDA) would make all business owners, including daycares and schools, subject to costly lawsuits for refusing to hire homosexuals, lesbians, or transgender individuals. In an open letter to the Gay, Lesbian, Bisexual and Transgender (LGBT) community Obama promised "As President, I will place the weight of my administration behind the enactment of the Matthew Shepard Act to outlaw hate crimes and a fully inclusive Employment Non-Discrimination Act to outlaw workplace discrimination on the basis of sexual orientation and gender identity."

http://www.bilerico.com/2008/02

open_letter_from_barack_obama_to_the_lgb.php

Barack Obama Believes that "Traditional View" of Scripture is Associated with Homophobia

Obama has been widely praised by gay leaders for his willingness to chastise Black clergy who refuse to condone homosexuality. Regarding Black Christian attitudes toward homosexuality, Obama said, "...the African-American community is more churched and most African-American churches are still fairly traditional in their interpretations of Scripture. And so from the pulpit or in sermons you still hear homophobic attitudes expressed. And since African-American ministers are often the most prominent figures in the African-American community those attitudes get magnified or amplified a little bit more than in other communities."

http://www.advocate.com/exclusive_detail_id53285_Page3.asp

Barack Obama "Strongly Disagrees" with Pastor Donnie McClurkin's View of Homosexuality

When campaigning in some southern states, Barack Obama employed musician and preacher, Donnie McClurkin, who has publicly testified about his deliverance from homosexuality. This infuriated homosexual activists, and Obama responded to the pressure by clarifying that he strongly disagrees with McClurkin's belief that homosexuals can change, and added a gay minister to the tour. Read his interview about the incident here: http://www.advocate.com/ news_detail_ektid50021.asp

Barack Obama Strongly Supports the Abortion Agenda

According to the U.S. Center for disease control, 1,450 Black children are aborted each day in America. Since 1973, when abortion was legalized, more than 14 million Black babies have been killed in the Black woman's womb. More than twice as many Blacks have died from abortion than from heart disease, cancer, accidents, violent crimes and AIDS combined.

> **Abortion is the number one killer of Black Americans**

In a February news conference, Day Gardner, President of the National Black Pro-life Union said:

"Abortion is a racist, genocidal act. African Americans should not ignore abortion when they vote. Abortion is the number one killer of Black Americans — killing more Black people than all other deaths combined. Yet there are Black men and women who stand in support of the vicious killing of our smallest children — all in order to win popularity contests or for the coveted prize of becoming the first Black president of the United States. The focus must always be foremost [on] the children who are killed by abortion and the women who suffer through the ordeal. And we must make sure that political figures know this fact — if you are for abortion, then we are not for you, no matter what color your skin is."

At the same conference, Alveda King agreed:

"We can talk about poverty; we can talk about the war; we can talk about teen pregnancy; we can talk about incarceration. However, if we're not allowed to live, we'll never encounter those issues." http://www.blackchristiannews.com/aa-leaders_call_blacks_to_act_against_abortion.html

Barack Obama received a 100% rating from NARAL for 2005, 2006 and 20007 (Source: NARAL.org)

Barack Obama voted NO on prohibiting minors to cross states lines for an abortion (S.403 Child Interstate Abortion Notification Act)

Barack Obama is against a ban on Partial Birth Abortion

"Obama criticized the Supreme Court ruling in April that upheld a ban on a late-term abortion procedure opponents call 'partial-birth' abortion. Obama said the ruling 'dramatically departs from previous precedents safeguarding the health of pregnant women.' He was not in the Senate in 2003 when the bill was voted on originally." http://asp.usatoday.com/news/politics/election2008/issues.aspx?i=9&c=12

Barack Obama Will Appoint Supreme Court Nominees to Uphold Roe v. Wade

At a forum in July conducted by the Planned Parenthood Action Fund, Obama implied that he would appoint Supreme Court nominees who support Roe v. Wade, the 1973 decision legalizing abortion.

'With one more vacancy on the court, we could be looking at a majority hostile to a woman's fundamental right to choose for the first time since Roe v. Wade, and that is what is at stake in this election," Obama said. "It is time for a different attitude in the White House. It is time for a different attitude in the Supreme Court'."
http://asp.usatoday.com/news/politics/election2008/issues.aspx?i=9&c=12

Should the Black American community assumptively buy into the idea that Obama cares about them, the one sure way to know if this is true would be to examine his intentions of preserving the future of those people. Consider this:

"Barack does not seem to care that 40% of the abortions in America are performed on Black women resulting in a virtual genocide of Blacks in the country. Because of his callous position [emphasis mine] on this issue, and his fervent desire to protect the right of a woman to be exploited, abused and even killed by these methods, he has declared that he will appoint judges who feel the same way he does. This is in spite of the fact that every single Republican judicial nomination goes through a gauntlet of impossible, improbable questions that point blank, ask how they would vote on a case that would involve abortion, and if they would work to overturn Roe v. Wade. If they do not adhere to the liberal position on abortion, they can usually not even make it out of committee, and if they do make it out, they lose to a Democrat majority.

With Barack as president, with a Democrat controlled house and senate, it is a certainty that pro-abortion judges will be appointed. Liberal judges, like Ruth Bader Ginsberg, who have been waiting for a Barack to be elected before retiring, will usher in a new generation of people who ignore the original intent of the Constitution which is to protect the lives of all citizens, born and unborn, and provide for the right to life, liberty and the pursuit of happiness".

Nina May is the Founder and Chairman of the Renaissance Foundation, an international leadership organization with offices in the U.S. and the Republic of Korea. www.renaissancefoundation.us

Barack Obama Voted Against Protecting Infants Born Alive During Abortions

While a state senator in Illinois, Obama was the ONLY senator to give a speech on the senate floor against the Born Alive Infant Act which said that homo sapiens that were completely outside the mother's uterus, possessing a "beating heart, pulsation of the umbilical cord or definite movement of voluntary muscles" were "persons" and thus entitled to medical care. The legislation was proposed in 2001 in response to nurses' depositions saying that babies born accidentally during abortions were allowed to die of neglect in utility closets. Obama voted against this legislation four separate times.

This position places him radically to the left of even the staunchest pro-choice advocates in Congress, since the U.S. Senate passed legislation with identical language 98 to 0. Senator Obama's speech against the legislation is in the Illinois Senate record (Obama's testimony begins on page 85.) http://www.ilga.gov/senate/transcripts/strans92/ST033001.pdf

Barack Obama Believes Religion Does Not Allow Compromise and Therefore is Dangerous

"Politics depends on our ability to persuade each other of common aims based on a common reality. It involves the compromise, the art of what's possible. At some fundamental level, religion does not allow for compromise. It's the art of the impossible. If God has spoken, then followers are expected to live up to God's edicts, regardless of the consequences. To base one's life on such uncompromising commitments may be sublime, but to base our policy making on such commitments would be a dangerous thing" – Barack Obama in his *Call to Renewal* Speech, June 28, Washington, DC.

Black Americans are more likely to espouse a religion than Whites. Thirteen percent of Whites in America say they have no religion, while only 3 percent of Black Americans say they have no religion. Two-thirds of Black Americans identify themselves as evangelical Christians, twice the number of Whites. According to the Pew Forum on Religion & Public Life, U.S. Religious Landscape Survey, (February 2008): "On matters of religious faith, the Religious Landscape Survey report released in February found that among all major racial and ethnic groups in the United States, African Americans are the most likely to report a formal religious affiliation. Fully 85% of Black adults report belonging to one or another Christian denomination, mostly Protestant. (78%) Even among those who are unaffiliated, 70% of Blacks belong to the "religious unaffiliated" category (that is, they say that religion is either somewhat or very important in their lives), compared with slightly more than one-third of the unaffiliated population overall." http://pewresearch.org/pubs/895/obamas-Black-audience

Barack Obama Places Politics and Culture Above Christianity

"Even those who claim the Bible's inerrancy make distinctions between Scriptural edicts, sensing that some passages—the Ten Commandments, say, or a belief in Christ's divinity—are central to Christian faith, while others are more culturally specific and may be modified to accommodate modern life.

The American people intuitively understand this, which is why the majority of Catholics practice birth control and some of those opposed to gay marriage nevertheless are opposed to a Constitutional amendment to ban it. Religious leadership need not accept such wisdom in counseling their flocks, but they should recognize this wisdom in their politics" –Barack Obama in his *Call to Renewal* Speech – June 28, 2008 Washington, DC

Barack Obama Believes in Salvation Without Jesus

Barack Obama has publicly stated that belief in Jesus is not necessary for salvation. He has said that he believes Islam is just as valid a path to God as Christianity and that his late mother, who was not a Christian, is in heaven because she was a good person.
http://www.onenewsnow.com/Election2008/Default.aspx?id=73553

The Obamas Do Not Tithe

The Obamas gave significantly less than 10% of their income to charity, even after book deals made them millionaires in 2005. The Obamas' Income Tax returns indicate they gave the following percentages of their adjusted gross income to charity: 2006: 6.1%, 2005: 4.7%, 2004: 1.2%, 2003: 1.4%, 2002: 0.4%, 2001: 0.5%, 2000: 0.9%; in their lowest earning year during this time period their adjusted gross income was over $250,000.
http://elections.foxnews.com/2008/03/25/obamas-open-tax-returns-earned-nearly-1m-in-2006/

According to a 2003 study entitled, "How Americans Give, The Chronicle of Philanthropy," 90 percent of charitable donations given by African Americans is to churches or other religious institutions. Church-based giving accounts for the bulk of African-American charitable donations. Anyone within the Black American community that is a pastor or leader should have cause for concern when viewing the Obamas' record of "charitable" giving. "CHARITY"! (Donations, Please! By Angelia Dickens | TheRoot.com)

Barack Obama Opposes School Choice

In a speech to the American Federation of Teachers, Barack Obama emphatically told the teacher's union that he does not support private school vouchers, saying "We need to focus on fixing and improving our public schools, not throwing our hands up and walking away from them." www.nysun.com/new-york/obama-tells-teachers-union-he-opposes-vouchers/81801/

Approximately 89 percent of Black Americans would send their child to private school if they received vouchers. According to Jay P. Greene, senior fellow at the Manhattan Institute and endowed head of the Department of Education Reform at the University of Arkansas:

> **89 percent of Black Americans would send their child to private school if they received vouchers.**

"In addition to evidence about the competitive effects of voucher programs, studies done in Arizona, Michigan, and Texas show that competition from charter schools improves the academic performance of nearby traditional public schools. A fairly large body of research also exists on the effects of public school districts' competing with each other." http://www.city-journal.org/2008/forum0124.html

In a study on private school voucher programs in Milwaukee, Cleveland, New York and Washington, Paul Peterson of Harvard's Kennedy School found:

"According to the test score results, African American students from low-income families who switch from a public school to a private school do considerably better after two years than students who do not receive a voucher opportunity. However, students from other ethnic background seem to learn after two years as much but no more in private schools than their public counterparts."

As for "throwing our hands up and walking away" from public schools, that is exactly what Senator Obama did when it came time to choose a school for his two daughters, who go to a private school. All voucher advocates are saying is that parents who don't have the wealth of the Obama's nonetheless deserve the same option to educate their children that the Senator and his wife have.

Examining Obama's statements, I think we can safely say he has an unwavering commitment to the destruction of Black American families. My friends, we have been here before. Obama's agenda is one that history has confirmed time and again as being hostile toward the Black American family and detrimental to our advancement.

Barack Obama & Christianity

The power of religion is found in the freedom the worshipper has to embrace it. Recall the words of Jesus Christ:

But the hour cometh, and now is, when the true worshippers shall worship the Father in spirit and in truth: for the Father seeketh such to worship him. God is a Spirit: and they that worship him must worship him in spirit and in truth. - John 4:23, 24

True faith that is undefiled before God, does not involve the interference, persuasion, or coercion of men. It is a movement of the Spirit that operates on a mysterious level where a bond is created by man's spirit being invoked by God's Spirit. The individual then willingly yields to God and a relationship is established. Conversely, that person may elect to reject this wooing of the heart and a relationship is *not* established. It is an individual choice of the individual within his or her own heart and mind; it is not a law that can be imposed upon the individual by any government.

As Christians, we believe this experience of finding one's faith takes place through the mediation of Jesus Christ—by His death (for our transgressions) and resurrection (for our redemption). There is wisdom that comes to us through faith and it can be easily identified. It is written in James 3:14-18:

But if ye have bitter envying and strife in your hearts, glory not, and lie not against the truth. This wisdom descendeth not from above, but is earthly, sensual, devilish. For where envying and strife is, there is confusion and every evil work. But the wisdom that is from above is first pure, then peaceable, gentle, and easy to be intreated, full of mercy and good fruits, without partiality, and without hypocrisy. And the fruit of righteousness is sown in peace of them that make peace.

On his recent "international campaign swing" that included a stop in the Holy Land, Barack Obama suggested it is necessary to create harmony between all religions in order to have peace. To this I would respond that peace is not contingent upon all of us believing the same thing. Peace comes when we respect one another's differences. What we need in the Middle East is a secure environment where people can practice...well, freedom of religion. In this country our Founding Fathers singled out freedom of religion as a fundamental right of all people. To advance the idea of harmony is fine; but the crux of the issue is *security for people of all faiths —no matter if they are Christian, Jew or Muslim —to worship as they please.*

Barack Obama's "Oneness Doctrine" potentially violates not only the foundations of our nation, but the First Amendment. By attempting to create a governmental state of peace through religious rhetoric, non-recognition of different faiths and lack of protection for those who worship. Obama comes dangerously close to trampling on the First Amendment, which states:

Congress shall make no law respecting an establishment of religion, or prohibiting the free exercise thereof...

Star Parker, columnist on World Net Daily, said it this way:

"It may come as a surprise to Obama, but for Christians, for Muslims and for Jews, their differences do not amount to barriers to a better world but sources of meaning that define themselves and the world.

They want to be Christians, Muslims and Jews. They just want protection. They want to be able to be who they are and live peacefully and securely. Those disturbing this security are the problem. Not the differences.

Which gets to Mr. Obama's very problematic idea about freedom.

He does not seem to grasp that the beauty of freedom is its respect for differences and creation of conditions, legal and political, that allow them to exist, flourish and provide benefits to all. In fact, politicians with agendas to "unify," who think they know who and what everyone should be, are invariably those who threaten freedom."

Star Parker is President and Founder of CURE, the Coalition on Urban Renewal & Education Visit her at: http://www.urbancure.org

God is a Spirit and He seeks such to worship Him. No man can teach another man to know God. Knowing God is a deeply personal journey that comes to each person in a different way. I happen to believe that God reveals Himself through Jesus Christ alone. This is the one true way. As long as I am free to believe what I choose to believe, and others are free to do the same, we can acknowledge our differences and maintain harmony. But you don't create harmony by advancing an agenda that seeks to make good people believe the same thing.

Barack Obama was caught saying something he believes. At a San Francisco fundraiser, away from the prying eyes of the press, Obama reflected on why small-town voters in Pennsylvania and the Midwest seem resistant to his appeal. He said those areas had lost jobs for 25 years. Therefore, people "get bitter, they cling to guns or religion or antipathy to people who aren't like them or anti-immigrant sentiment or anti-trade sentiment as a way to explain their frustrations."

"The Underside of Hope", Rich Lowry of National Review On-line, April 15, 2008 http://article.nationalreview.com/?q=NGFjZDlkOWZmNGQxMDUxNzQ1NTNiMDFhMDZiY2FiMmU

Obama has apologized for his phrasing while defending the substance of his statement. And why not? He was recalling an article of left-wing orthodoxy going back centuries: that the working class is distracted by religion and other peripheral concerns from focusing on its economic interests and embracing socialism.

Versions of Obama's insight have been expounded by a world-famous nineteenth century economist (Karl Marx), by a 1960s New Left philosopher (Herbert Marcuse) and by a best-selling contemporary liberal writer (Thomas Frank, author of *What's the Matter With Kansas?*), among many others. The other "First Black President", Bill Clinton, wrote in his memoir that Republicans wanted to undermine confidence in government so voters would be more receptive to "their strategy of waging campaigns on divisive social and cultural issues like abortion, gay rights, and guns."

Consider Obama's formulation. He makes it sound like no one would be a hunter or a Christian absent economic distress; that economic circumstances drive people into such atavistic habits. The assumption is that only liberal attitudes are normal and well adjusted. If only these small-town people could earn more income, get an advanced degree, and move to a major metropolitan area, then they could shed their chrysalis of social conservatism."

I don't know about you, but my journey of faith has nothing to do with the government. I don't turn to God; I worship God. What's more, I trust Him to love me, lead me, and always be there for me. To elites like Barack Obama, government is more important than God. Or, put another way, Barack Obama believes that if government were doing its job none of us would need God. Then we could kiss this antiquated "belief in God thing" goodbye and become like him...a sophisticated citizen of the world who understands that a well-run government is all it takes.

I can see it now on the evening news:

**Barack Obama proposes new legislation
requiring that men love their wives.**

**Barack Obama today announced a new government initiative to
help teach mothers to love their
children and children to obey their parents.**

**Barack Obama today called upon Congress to draft new
legislation that will cause millions to forsake their culture,
traditions, and beliefs to embrace a new universal concept of God
that he insists, "everyone can get behind for the sake of harmony."**

I do not believe Obama really understands what he is asserting. Then maybe I'm wrong. He certainly has the right to believe that it is the truth as much as I have the right to believe it is not. And we are FREE to be right and FREE to be wrong. I can live with that, can he? Obviously not. He is determined to make his way the law of the land, totally ignoring true democracy—the right of the people.

It's going to be tough sledding even for Barack Obama if he thinks government can legislate the spirit of men. I think Star Parker's point is well taken. Politicians with an agenda, who think they know what is best for the rest of us, particularly in matters of faith, often end up doing more harm than good.

More government simply encroaches upon civilized people. Such thinking is a brand of socialistic domination. We've done just fine these past 225 plus years, Mr. Obama, and the future looks bright without your anti-American religious views, whose DNA is rooted in a rotten dogma of Marxism and socialistic regimes that have destroyed civilizations.

As far as the Christian faith is concerned, we believe our God draws men and women to believe in Him through loving kindness and the promise of salvation, not government funded programs. We also believe in loving our neighbors as ourselves and even loving our enemies. To love our enemies is to confront them with what we believe to be the truth, with boldness and without condemnation. Should we remain passive and compliant in order to get along with and tolerate the ungodly and the immoral? Or, are we called by God to point out when people we love, or even complete strangers, make bad and even evil choices? It is not incumbent upon us as men and women of faith to advance the positive solution we know will remedy these poor choices. And that, of course, is turning to God. Surely, it is expected of us as Christians to respect persons of other faiths. Again, our nation is a free nation, which is why many have reached our shores to flee religious persecution.

Barack Obama's side of the political spectrum embodies the continued drift in our society away from God. Rather than adhering to a belief in a higher power—as our Founding Fathers did and referenced in all our founding documents—today our society is being systematically pulled from that tradition.

I know full well I am not alone in my concern about where this is leading us.

I am one who believes God set this country in place to be a beacon of light for all mankind. Yes, it has taken us time to get where we are. Being human, we Americans are fallible. We have never claimed to be otherwise. No one can deny we are a melting pot of good people, always purposefully pushing forward to perfect our imperfect nation—under God.

Why then is there an ongoing assault on the faith of our fathers and the nation that was built and has prospered under these universal defining principles? Consider some of today's headlines:

Family Ordered to Remove Nativity Scene from Yard

NOVI (AP) - A Christmas time turf battle is being waged in suburban Detroit. A Novi family has been ordered to remove a seven-piece nativity scene from the front yard of their home, or face possible fines of $25 to $100 per week.

Group Wants Nativity Scene Removed in Green Bay

Dec 12, 2007

GREEN BAY, Wis. (AP) — The Green Bay City Council president paid for a nativity scene to be put up at City Hall after learning of an anti-religion group's protest of one in Peshtigo.

Turning from the God that our Founding Fathers worshipped is a critical step in redefining what America is as a nation. And this cannot be good. I think there are those who would like nothing better than to see America redefine itself and jettison all sense of God as our Creator, mentor and guiding light. One cannot deny that a powerful positive force has seemed to watch over America and guide her—through times of trial and peril. God has truly blessed America.

Whether what we are experiencing today is intentionally orchestrated or not is for you to decide. I submit watering down our faith and abandoning our sense that God is with us is one more step in making us question our motives as a nation. It makes us question whether or not we are a united people. It makes us focus on our differences rather than on the things we have in common. It makes us doubt our American exceptionalism. It erodes and weakens our "can do" attitude. It fosters the notion that our best days as a society and as a nation are behind us.

> **God has truly blessed America.**

I cannot comment on Barack Obama's spiritual beliefs, but I question why he has aligned himself with those who refuse to praise our virtues as Black Americans and as a nation, and who constantly condemn America for any and every perceived imperfection. Has his association with such individuals in any way distorted his view of our country and our people?

Throughout our journey, Americans have paid a price for the nation we have forged. Without a doubt, some more than others. Without question, our process of evolving as a good and just society has been fraught with trial and error. Still, I believe good triumphs over evil, and I believe more often than not, we Americans get it right.

One needs only to sit for a quiet moment and read Lincoln's Gettysburg Address.

Personally, I choose to see us as a united people who are basically good. Our foundation, the common American experience, is based on extraordinary principles of faith in God, the power of the family unit, and a system of laws that protect our individual rights.

I fear—yes, fear—Barack Obama because I do not know who he really is and, frankly, he is doing little to fully reveal himself. I am left only to speculate on what he believes and how he really views America. He is more inclined to apologize for America than standup for our unmatched record of generosity and a force for good in the world.

Defending his decision to refuse to wear a flag pin, Obama said while in Cedar Rapids, Iowa, "I decided I won't wear that pin on my chest. Instead I'm going to try to tell the American people what I believe what will make this country great and hopefully that will be a testimony to my patriotism."

> **The battle we are striving to win as Black Americans has less to do with government...**

He is enabled with an oratory that sounds so good but unfortunately rings hollow. I am left to wonder if Barack Obama believes in his heart—as I do in mine—that *we are* an exceptional nation. Does he fully grasp that our foundation as Black Americans is based on loving God, keeping His commandments and nurturing strong families? His pandering rhetoric emphasizes big government as the panacea to every problem, pain or predicament. I reject this. Our own personal resilience, with an uncompromising faith in God, is the only true way forward for all Americans. The battle we are striving to win as

Black Americans has less to do with government and more to do with personal resolve to get an education and develop a bankable skill.

Before any man or woman can effectively lead this nation, they must first have a deep resolve and a strong sense of who they are, not how they wish others to see them. Barack Obama loves the adulation of the crowds, but I do not sense he has a core of values and principles that ground him with the fundamental beliefs of both the majority of Black and White Americans. How then can he inspire us in the things that really matter to us? He can't!

Perhaps you sense it too. We need to be honest with ourselves. There is a kind of disconnect between us as Black Americans and Barack Obama. Perhaps it is because we sense Barack Obama is a political marionette—a "ringer" being used by others to further an agenda which has historically hurt us. Perhaps these "elites" have determined they can leverage Barack Obama and attain power through the Black vote. By putting forward a Black face are they expecting Black Americans to automatically buy in without inspecting?

As of yet, Barack Obama has not proven that he is his own man. It is entirely plausible that powerful forces behind the scenes see an opportunity to put Obama in the Oval Office and then move him around like a pawn at their bidding. We would shake our heads in disbelief if we knew the true agenda they plan for America. I'll go farther than that. With Barack Obama and his handlers in office, within a few years you and I won't even recognize America. The valueless agenda advanced by the liberal forces in this country is counter to the will of the majority of Americans. The polls confirm this time and again. But if they can grab power through an assumed Black American, they will turn this nation in a direction that will cause grave harm to you, your family, and our country.

Consider this:

"Barack Obama is in the chorus of liberal Democrats who continually oppose strict constructionists who want to honor the original intent of the Constitution instead of seeing it as a "living, breathing document" that takes on the cultural nuances of the day. It is not surprising though that they still hold that view of the Constitution after more than 100 years of applying their own interpretations to very clear and concise Amendments to the Constitution. It is surprising though, that a Black man, who wants to be president, would buy into that position since it was the politically motivated interpretations of the Constitution that prevented total and complete racial integration. And ironically, the penumbra of equal protection, which was opposed on its face by Democrats to allow Blacks equal access to all benefits of American citizenship, is the very foundation of the legal process of abortion, which finds 40% of its victims being Black babies."   *Nina May*

Barack Obama is a well-polished and highly attractive empty suit. He has dashed on the political scene so fast; none of us can ascertain who he is and what he really believes because he has offered little substance in the midst of much stardom. And yet he is poised to become the next President of the United States, the leader of the free world. There are many of us who are deeply concerned about what will result from a Barack Obama presidency. Our best interests as Black Americans—as patriotic Americans—lie in a new direction that reflects our core beliefs and values, not merely a resemblance of someone we look like.

CHAPTER TWO

Preserving Our Foundation

If the foundations be destroyed, what can the righteous do?

Psalms 11:3

The foundation of the Black people has always been God and family. We are resilient in our ability to face opposition and setbacks while maintaining an optimistic spirit. Do we not always say, "It'll be alright. Just hang in there. God is faithful"? Or, "You know God won't let you fall. But if you do, He'll always be there to pick you up"? All the old Negro spirituals were born out of oppression and suppression. And what a stirring body of music it is. These wonderful songs – which emerge almost mystically from deep within our collective conscious—are an important cultural legacy and a constant reminder of the price that was paid by our ancestors.

In examining our history, there are three key elements that form a firm foundation upon which our people have been able to endure and persevere:

(1) Personal courage

(2) Unshakable faith in God

(3) The ability to create and sustain a close-knit family

These values are just as important today, as in the troubled times of our past. They are the fundamentals that give one's life meaning, and from which we derive personal fulfillment and success. Arguably, these are the only things that have value…the only things that truly matter.

Personal Courage

No one can deny that as Black Americans we have exhibited great personal courage and fortitude throughout our journey. When I speak of "courage", I am really talking about a condition of the heart, the kind of personal resilience that comes from deep within us, and is predicated on a core set of values that transcend race, gender, and molecular DNA.

Courage is as personal as one's breath. It is as unique as the retina in one's eye. It is there inside us because God has given every one of us the gift of the ability to be courageous. And dare I say it, courage, when taken to full value, can result in martyrdom. If a man or woman knows beyond a doubt that what they believe in their hearts is true, they can confront any hardship, suffer any pain, or endure any persecution.

This is why God is central to the Black American community.

It is hard to stand tall and remain courageous in any circumstance if you have no core belief system. Old Negro spirituals, along with today's songs, speak volumes of how we endured and made it. It wasn't government or that of a king amongst men that gave us hope for change through oppressive times of the past. It was the single hope that God would send deliverance from our suffering in songs like, "Swing low sweet chariot ...coming for to carry me home."

Each and every time adversity strikes home, our hearts' cry has always been, "LORD JESUS HELP RIGHT NOW." The very presence of Black people in the Bible is a testament that our walk of faith and reliance upon God alone has enabled us to overcome century after century of oppression. He will not forsake us, however, history shows that when we choose foolishly, we permit the consequences of our decision to be ours to bear. When we turn from Him, when the ice gets thin, our courage wavers, and we embrace false gods and exchange our votes for hollow promises.

Courage should also not be confused with blind allegiance. Courage requires knowledge and insight—and ultimately wisdom. Who among us are courageous enough to challenge what the "group" thinks? Who among us will speak out and say "no" if they feel their friends, neighbors, loved ones and fellow citizens are in danger of being deceived and ultimately injured economically, socially, and even physically?

If we are to preserve our country, we must do so with the same level of courage it took the pilgrims to sail across an unknown sea to a desolate rocky coastline and establish a fragile foothold on the edge of a vast and hostile land. Or, as Black Americans have done, sustain our courage, our dignity, and yes, our sense of humor throughout our long crucible to wrest a rightful place in the American firmament.

Today, we have a different set of challenges. And they will require no less courage to defy what is wrong morally, ethically, and, yes, Constitutionally, than it did to start a nation, breathe the breath of freedom into it, and ultimately, keep it safe and on course under the founding principles that have served us so well.

According to *The New York Times*, for the first time ever a majority of American women, 51%, are living without a husband. For Black women, the number is even higher, around 70%. The out-of-wedlock birthrate for Black Americans is close to a staggering 70%. Are Black Americans abandoning the traditional family structure?

The usual apologists bleat, "Oh, the numbers do not tell the whole story." They try to excuse this with suggestions it has something to do with our mobile society, similar to the dislocation of Black Americans moving north after World War II.

My friends, we are never going to confront and solve this problem by passing it off as some kind of demographic trend or electing a president based solely on his skin color. Nor can we say this is the result of White people trying to hurt us or our government is not doing enough. No. *We are doing this to ourselves. We fail to be self-governing within our own homes. Courage takes a willingness to see and ultimately embrace what is true.*

I feel it is my solemn duty to call out to Black Americans to resist choosing expedient blackness over courage…courage to see what is true and what is a lie. I further call out to the Black Church to mend its ways. Perhaps it is time to stop preaching Jesus' message while at the same time supporting a completely contrary message dished out to our people by power hungry politicians. Ask yourself the tough questions, without consideration of skin color. Do you honestly believe what Barack Obama and his party intend to do will be good for you, your family, and your country?

The long road of our history as a people leads us to this moment. These are perilous times for you and me as Black Americans. Putting our current circumstance in the context of my Christian faith, I believe the battle is upon us and it comes down to this—truth or lie. Are we able to confront what is before our eyes and recognize what is true? Or, for the sake of expediency and pride are we accepting a lie?

It is going to take COURAGE to stand for truth. But when we do, we know God and will see that we have a measure of His strength to sustain us in the fight. We Americans are one tough bunch. Compassionate, of course, but also imbued, I believe, with a noble character. We learn from our mistakes. We move on. Always trying our best to get it right. Americans inspire, and we Black Americans are on every page of our nation's epic story.

Unshakable Faith in God

If my people who are called by my name, shall humble themselves, and pray, and seek my face, and turn from their wicked ways; then will I hear from heaven, and will forgive their sin, and will heal their land.

2 Chronicles 7:14

Let's face it; we are likely headed for tough times in America.

I choose to look at it as a natural and necessary process, one that has been repeated time and again through the ages. It is the way God works when His people have strayed too far. He pulls us up short, and, although it may be painful, we will be called to account, and be challenged as a nation to rediscover our trust and faith in God.

Our unshakable faith in God, our very foundation, will enable us to be truly free, never again allowing any man or government to control our lives, our destiny. I am convinced that this is the fullness of time for us as Black Americans. This is the time—the age—in which we truly break free from the shackles we have allowed ourselves to wear.

> In essence, there must be a battle – a fight, if you will, for righteousness.

In essence, there must be a battle—a fight, if you will, for righteousness. As a Christian, I see the coming storm as just that—a battle. Not the clash of arms, but certainly two armies locked in a spiritual battle between the forces of good and the forces of evil. In our rational minds, we tend to discount the concept of evil, questioning if such an organized effort is even possible. Is Satan out there? Does he control the actions of men to the extent that a vast army of followers can twist the fate of mankind? Is God calling upon His people—the ones who speak His name—to stand up and be counted? As Christians, we know this to be so. And though afraid, we embrace the coming storm.

Black Americans have demonstrated tremendous faith and resilience in the face of powers beyond our control that continually seem to align against us and hold us in captivity. How else can you explain it? Here we are in the 21st Century still wrestling, struggling if you will, with many of the same challenges we have always faced. They never seem to go away. Without an unshakable faith in God, are we not in danger of repeating a huge mistake—over and over again?

Rather than wholeheartedly embracing the foundation God wants us to build upon, we look for a "king among men" to come to our rescue. With a silver tongue they are able to twist us around and persuade us that, if we will only trust in them, "everything will be all right." They, at last, are the ones we have been waiting for.

Barack Obama fits this mold perfectly. He typifies an image that allows us to put a face on what we are most desperate for: *deliverance.* But can Barack Obama really do this? Put another way, do you believe God wants us to put our faith and trust in the Barack Obamas of this world for our deliverance? Or do you think it is reasonable to suggest that God expects us to stop repeating the same mistake over and over again and instead turn to Him—and in so doing sew the true means of our deliverance from within ourselves?

I, for one, have come to this point in my journey.

If Barack Obama is elected President, he will unabashedly usher in an era of socialism. His social and economic agenda will be enacted and forced down our throats like nothing we have ever seen in the history of this country.

And where will this leave us, my friends? It will leave us as Black Americans in the same exact place we have always been. Once again we will see our great hopes dashed upon the rocks of false and empty political promises. Moreover, we stand to reap the brunt of the back-lash that is sure to ensue from the pain it will bring to our nation.

Sooner or later God will pull us up short. Perhaps He is preparing to do just that through Barack Obama. Perhaps He is getting ready to say to us, "When, my children, will you ever learn? False kings and false promises have held you down." Perhaps the clash of good and evil is upon us, and we are now being called upon to choose.

In the context of my Christian faith, I believe that from the beginning the enemy of all mankind, Satan, has fought against the foundation of all that is good. Yes, I believe there are absolutes. Good and evil. God and Satan. Anytime there is an attack against the foundation of any-thing that is good, it is brought on by the presence of evil.

Consider how Barack Obama's objectives directly attack the foun-dation of the Black community. Do not the positions he is espousing fundamentally undermine the very things that are good in our lives and that strengthen us? Is this intentional on his part or is evil work-ing its way into our souls? You know as well as I, that people can be used to establish evil systems and not necessarily be inherently evil themselves. Then again, at some point it comes down to this: A per-son chooses to go against the conscience that God has given every person. It's called free will. I believe in that small voice inside us—if we choose to pray and listen—that tells us when we are doing right...or doing wrong.

Another powerful Scriptural phrase comes to mind...

Speaking lies in hypocrisy; having their conscience seared with a hot iron;
1 Timothy 4:2

Barack Obama is by political definition a liberal. One of the prob-lems I have found in trying to have a meaningful discussion with people who have a politically liberal worldview is that they often abandon reason. Often is really an understatement. After the third or fourth statement, they have to abandon reason. I see this happening with the hyped adulation of Barack Obama. To me, facts matter. The Gospel of Jesus Christ matters. There are indeed absolutes. There is right and there is wrong. There is good and there is evil. When confronted with facts—or a belief system rooted in the Christian faith—liberals freeze up. When they cannot refute the truth, they react emotionally. This is certainly the case when you begin to talk about our foundation as Black Americans.

To a person of the liberal persuasion, the foundation is whatever they want it to be. God's will for mankind—the foundation he has laid down for each of us—is for them, an inconvenient truth. They want no boundaries, no judgments with regard to their actions. The old 1960s saying comes to mind, "If it feels good do it." Or the even more banal conceit, "…as long as I'm not hurting anyone else." Listen to that small voice. Our actions have consequences—for our children, our families, and our fellow citizens. Should not our belief system, our foundation, be contrasted with Barack Obama's ideas for America and Black Americans in particular?

Forget emotion when it comes to Barack Obama. You and I as Black Americans cannot afford to be conned by slick packaging and emotionally charged speeches. I am calling upon my generation of men and women to refuse this wicked norm. We must look deeper. One sure way to get at the truth—if we are willing to accept it as God reveals it—is to contrast what Barack Obama espouses with our foundation as Black Americans.

Do not be afraid. You must give voice to your convictions. You must listen to that small voice. God is speaking to you of what is right and wrong, and what is truth and what is a lie. As you learn to embrace this wisdom, you must also learn to give it public expression. What do I mean by this? As Black Americans we have an innate fear of speaking out against our leaders when we disagree with them. We let them command the floor while our voices and opinions are never heard. We dare not say, "Pastor, with all due respect, I disagree with you." If the person is Black and popular, he (or she) is right. If that person gives money to our churches, he is right. If it is a politician making promises to get our vote, he is right.

I have stated what I believe to be our foundation as Black Americans. Referencing the Scriptures, I ask you, "If the foundations be destroyed, what can the righteous do?"

Now is the time to think hard. See what is true and what is not. I believe the battle is upon us. I am unwilling to join the parade and march in lockstep with delirious believers who think Barack Obama is their next redeemer. No. The time has come for us to turn away from the promise of easy answers, and confront what we know to be true within our hearts. Barack Obama is another in a long line of manipulators after our souls in the guise of votes. I will not give him mine. I trust in our foundation as Black Americans. I choose this path.

Creating and Sustaining a Close-Knit Family

What is a nation's greatest strength? I believe most of us would answer, her people, of course. Strong families are the heart and soul of any nation. Fracture and weaken the family unit and you have scored a direct hit on that country's core.

Is the Black American family stronger today than in years past? I could ask the same question of all American families of any race or nationality. But this discussion is focused on our Black American community.

Hardly a day passes when Selena and I don't engage in conversation with a worried mother or father who is deeply distressed by the constant barrage of utterly inappropriate messages that our children are exposed to day in and day out. They try hard to counter it with proper parenting, but they wonder if they are losing the fight. It's hard enough to feed, clothe and educate a family today, let alone worry about holding the line against a growing tide of negative and degrading output from an increasingly irresponsible entertainment industry.

No matter who you are, where you work, or how much money you have in the bank, I wager that for most people, their family is the most important thing. When you go to work each day, your overriding reason for doing so is to feed, clothe, shelter and educate your family. You view your children understanding they are the citizens of tomorrow. It is natural for men and women to find one another, fall in love, and have children. This is one of life's joys. It requires enormous commitment to be a good mother and father. There is every challenge you can imagine and more. It takes years to know if you have even done a good job, and sometimes you will never know. Still, it is how we carry on. It is how we build and sustain our country.

> **It requires enormous commitment to be a good mother and father.**

Creating and sustaining healthy and stable families should be a no-brainer; but the weakening of the family structure—particularly in the Black community—has led to enormous problems. If we really want better lives for Black Americans going forward, we must concentrate more on doing the heavy lifting in our homes.

If you and I really appreciated our heritage the way we claim to, we would work harder and smarter and with greater courage to put a stop to the destructive habits that we have allowed to poison our communities. The evidence is overwhelming and irrefutable: a strong family is the best safeguard against poverty and despair. I want to again point out that any hope we may have in Barack Obama is misplaced. The real hope and change we desire starts at home.

When you and I look at the Black American family, what do we see? One of the first things we see is the absence of fathers. Fathers sustain families through hard work and doing what is right to keep everyone safe, healthy and happy. Without fathers, children are left with one less role model and more likely to live in poverty. The dangerous levels of unwed mothers and illegitimate children are also a grave concern to the Black American community. Study after study has shown that children born out of wedlock are more likely to live in poverty, use drugs, commit suicide and drop out of school.

As Black American mothers and fathers, we must rethink why we are voting for Barack Obama. If you are not spending quality time in the lives of your children while keeping the flames of love alive with your spouse, what exactly are you expecting Barack Obama to do? Is another government initiative really going to solve anything?

It's not about politics outside of your home; it is how you deal with policy issues inside your home.

Creating, nurturing, and sustaining a strong and resilient family requires a committed, and yes, courageous, mother and father. It requires above all else two loving parents who stand together with an unshakable faith in God, and a willingness to work hard and persevere. You certainly do not have to wait for new laws to be passed, government subsidies to be granted, or yet another community initiative in order for your family to thrive. Waiting around for the government to do what you can do for yourself is self-defeating. Our

Black family formation is nearly dead in the water. We must look within ourselves and our foundation to change this.

Are you willing to spend time studying the issues, making yourself aware, and then conveying that information to family and friends? Will you resist the temptation to get a government handout for your community?

Ronald Reagan

As a businessman and church leader, I know one thing: Black Americans have a built in value system. They will say right to your face, "You know better!" And give you that Black American look. Should we not now give Barack Obama that look—assuming he would understand it? My colleagues and I in Black Americans for Real Change are sounding an alarm. We truly fear that if Barack Obama is in the White House, he will not just tamper with our Black American foundation, he will seek to irrevocably alter it. We simply cannot afford this.

The Godly Man and the Faithful

Help, LORD; for the godly man ceaseth; for the faithful fail from among the children of men.

Psalms 12:1

Lately I have been asking people who have an Obama sticker on their car or in their store window why they are voting for him. It's my little informal poll of potential Black American voters. I will tell you flat out, most could not give me a good solid answer because they don't really have a compass within themselves.

Not long ago I was in a coffee shop writing and I noticed a young man at a nearby table drawing in a notebook. Curious, I watched what he was doing and eventually struck up a conversation. One thing led to another and we began discussing politics. The level of trust he was willing to place in Barack Obama was startling. After much back and forth debate, I began to realize he was not a happy person. He felt a Barack Obama presidency would improve his lot in life. I finally looked him in the eye and asked him, "what exactly do you believe in?" He shook his head and said, "Nothing really."

He proceeded to tell me he felt Christians are always pointing fingers at others and telling them they are wrong. It occurred to me that people like him, who by their own words say they don't believe in anything, tend to accuse those that do believe in someone bigger than themselves, of being narrow-minded. I said to him, "If the Christian mind is narrow and we are happy, and your mind is broad and you are not happy, then why accuse the Christian of being wrong?"

It's amazing how God can light up your life and change your outlook and your life's condition if you let Him in. This unhappy young man was ready and willing to put all his faith in one mortal man, Barack Obama, to change his life because he had no belief system to sustain him.

Without godly men, faithful men, a country is doomed to be ruled by tyrannical men. The words of Barack Obama are designed to lull us to sleep with the idea of change and hope and a new and improved federal government. He has a tendency to talk down to us as Black Americans—treating us like children and our children as if they were his own. Black Americans can't afford to be pimped into thinking we have found a sugar daddy. We who place our trust in God Almighty already have a Father. He has given us His Spirit and we need not look to any man, including Barack Obama, to redeem us. This is a time when we must remain strong and resist such a person, no matter how charismatic he may be. Character over charisma must always be our choice. Especially yesterday, today and always.

Look back at our history. What has sustained us?

Personal Courage

An unshakable faith in God

The ability to create and sustain a close-knit family

If you are like me, you will be hard pressed to find very many Black Americans who do not believe in God through salvation in Jesus Christ—or at least know someone who believes within their immediate family. Certainly you have those who believe in other religions, but you can trace their experience right back to the God of Abraham, Isaac and Jacob. It is only recently that we have seen an exodus from the faith of our fathers to the path of humanism and to other religions.

As I follow the words and actions of Barack Obama, he does not appear to hold to the God of the Bible, although he claims otherwise. Only God knows Barack Obama's heart and his true motives. I am simply inspecting the fruit of a man who aspires to be our next President. He gives the impression of being a Christian as defined by the world, not a Christian as defined by the Word of God. And, not a Christian as defined by our Black American foundation.

My understanding of Obama would heighten if he emphatically stated he is not a Christian, rather than to claim he is and then attempt to redefine "Christian." If the God of the Bible is God then serve Him. If Baal is god then serve him. But please don't try to convince me you can serve two gods!

If you have a solid belief system – both political and spiritual –

you don't have to worry about always modifying your message. You know who you are. You know what you believe. You have no reason to constantly duck and hide. Where others see a masterful politician, I see a fraud. Where others see confidence, I see arrogance and a painful lack of humility. *To play the Black American card is to play Black Americans cheap.* To tinker with their Christian foundation is sinful and almost, if not completely, demonic. When you challenge the core beliefs of men, sooner or later they will arise and defend their faith, no matter the price.

CHAPTER THREE

Dr. Martin Luther King, Jr.
and Barack Obama
Side by Side

When I reflect on our Black American historical figures—what they believed in, what they stood up for, and what many of them died for—I am truly inspired. It is the greatest evidence of courage and leadership. These great men and women gave Black Americans a standard by which to judge real character, and modeled how to lead as an example by garnering knowledge from those we follow.

I feel exactly the opposite when I examine Barack Obama's words, philosophy and the disturbing cult of personality that surrounds him. I see crass showmanship in the guise of statesmanship. I see a shallow, empty vessel manipulating the legacy of our Black American luminaries who have gone before us for his own political gain.

As Black Americans, it is imperative we take time to read and study our rich history. We must refresh our collective memory before we cast our skin color behind the candidacy of Barack Obama. When you take the time do this, as I have, you will conclude that *Barack Obama is not representative of the Black American experience. He exists outside of it.* He has cleverly positioned himself to trade in on the Black American experience for the sole purpose of garnering votes in an attempt to establish a social order that does not reflect a FREE society. A sober reflection on what it means to be a Black American might cause you to consider the very real possibility that you are allowing yourself to be manipulated and used at the expense of your own dignity, intelligence, and hard won freedoms.

Let the voices of our ancestors open our eyes to who Barack Obama really is. To clarify our perception of what is true and real—and what is artifice and a lie. Dr. King advocated real change.

As I write this, it has been forty years since the famous summer of 1968. Today, Dr. Martin Luther King, Jr. is respected and honored by Blacks and Whites alike throughout America and, indeed, the world.

He was assassinated for expressing his hopes for the freedoms of all men. And for men to be validated by the content of their character rather than the color of their skin. The ideals he espoused have left their mark upon our American culture and society because his was an authentic voice for change at a time when change was sorely needed.

His voice rang true because what he believed in resonated deep within the smoldering conscience of the American people, Black and White. He challenged our society to belly up to the bar and honor our founding words, "All men are created equal." His moral certitude that our great nation must embrace equality and character over skin color was challenged, tested—and my friends—ultimately honored. He had a dream. And he changed things forever in America, for the good of us all.

Dr. King's voice was an authentic voice for real change, not an empty political slogan.

Please ask yourself, "Does Barack Obama really embody the Black American journey from Selma to this time and place?"

> ...do not sell your vote or your heritage to Barack Obama on the cheap.

If you are even the least bit unsure, do not sell your vote or your heritage to Barack Obama on the cheap.

Consider the following collection of notable quotes from the writings and speeches of Dr. King. Contrast these with the positions articulated by candidate, Barack Obama.

Dr. King: "A nation or civilization that continues to produce soft-minded men purchases its own spiritual death on the installment plan."

If nothing else, Senator Obama is a big government true believer. He is a Harvard graduate steeped in the theory and philosophy of an elite ivy-league school. He has little real-world experience and is basically a product of what he has been taught in a liberal university. That does not make him a deep thinker. What it has made him, like many who drink the liberal kool-aid in academia, is a liberal elitist.

Liberal elitists tend to believe they know best how others should live their lives. They smugly believe they have unique insight and that the rest of us are not educated enough or smart enough to manage our own lives. Their arrogance leads them to favor placing power in the hands of a few who make "benevolent" decisions on the false premise of the greatest good for the greatest number. In other words, Barack Obama is a socialist. He believes in wielding power over the people and their liberties.

Benevolent rule from above by Barack Obama and his elite advisors does not promote a competitive and productive community of confident Black American individuals, free to strive for their own definition of success. Rather, it fosters a kind of government-sanctioned twilight zone of permanent dependency, uncertainty, and predictable frustration. In essence, as Dr. King warned it brings a kind of spiritual death. I, for one, choose to heed Dr. King's warning about soft-minded men and reject the false "manna for votes" exchange promulgated by liberal politicians.

Barack Obama's agenda is a distortion of how human beings, and Black Americans specifically, learn, grow and ultimately find fulfillment. Think of the next generation of Black Americans (my children fall into this category). I shudder at the prospect of my children being systematically manipulated by a paternalistic government that dispenses crumbs in exchange for their votes. I want them to break free. To think for themselves. To trust in their foundation.

I say give people more power over their own lives and let them keep more of the money they earn. I am reminded of Patrick Henry's words rejecting the iron rule of the English monarchy, "Give me liberty or give me death." I listen to Barack Obama and his liberal cohorts and want to rise from my chair screaming, "Give me my foundation as a Black American and I'll take my chances!"

Dr. King: "Freedom is never voluntarily given by the oppressor; it must be demanded by the oppressed."
The Civil Rights Movement and the resulting Civil Rights Act of 1966 was a seminal moment in human history. It turns the stomach when elitists like Barack Obama continually throw Europe in our faces as though it were a bastion of racial tolerance, and our America—imperfect though she may be—as a benighted backwater that hates all people of color.

A recent article in *The New York Times* reported that there is, "One Black member representing constitutional France in the National Assembly among 555 members; no constitutional French senators out of some 300; only a handful of mayors out of some 36,000, and none from the poor Paris suburbs."

Citizen of the world, you say? I'll pass, Mr. Obama.

In 1968, forty years ago this summer, Black Americans were fully engaged in demanding total participation in American society. In 2006, a record number of Black Americans were serving in the United States Congress; 42 in the House of Representatives, including two delegates, and one Black American in the United States Senate.

We have made significant strides, yet we are continually oppressed by an institution (big government) that patronizes us; and strives to subjugate us into dependency and strip us of the very foundation that is the key to our success as Black Americans.

If we want REAL change it is time that we as Black Americans embrace a new paradigm—a new model. We must reject the false premise that government is our salvation; we must reject the smooth tongues of pandering politicians promising anything to get our votes. Real change starts from within each of us. Real change is predicated on returning to and relying on the tenants of our foundation—personal courage, an unshakable faith in God, and building and sustaining strong families.

Dr. King: "Everything that we see is a shadow cast by that which we do not see."

What do you see when you look at Barack Obama? I see a shadow of something that I cannot quite bring into focus. I am more uncomfortable still because I am unable to clearly see who is really behind him...controlling him. Do I believe there are forces at work doing just that? Take away the canned speeches and teleprompter and his comments are astonishingly simplistic and often portray a shocking naiveté.

Dare to question or apply critical thought in a public forum, and the response from his followers is instant and fierce. Consider the rather innocuous statement made by media success, Tavis Smiley. His statement on *The Tom Joyner Show* caused a firestorm:

"Just because Barack Obama is Black, doesn't mean he gets a pass on being held accountable on issues that matter to Black people," Smiley said.

I would say Tavis Smiley was stating the obvious. After all, we are in the process of electing the next President of the United States. Why should we want to give any candidate —Black or White—a pass? My grandmother would have heard Smiley's remark and said, "That's just common sense." What is happening to us?

Consider what Black American leaders like Dr. King, Frederick Douglass, Booker T. Washington and many others had to contend with in their time. These were men of intellect and ideas, phenomenal thinkers who truly challenged us and were fiercely challenged at the time. I am in awe of what they accomplished and under circumstances that we can only imagine.

My father, Bill Owens, Founder and President of Coalition of African-American Pastors (www.caapusa.org), has been a pioneer in forging a path toward relevance within the political struggle for Black Americans and White Americans as one. He passionately affirms the necessity of Black Americans staying with the values that has kept us strong, resilient, and together on most fundamental issues.

Rather than mindless cheering at his vacuous rhetoric, we should be looking at Barack Obama in an effort to penetrate through the shadows and ask, "Who is this guy?" "Do I really sense in him an *authentic* Black American voice?"

Dr. King: "An individual has not started living until he can rise above the narrow confines of his individualistic concerns to the broader concerns of all humanity."
Good and great men inspire us to be better than we would otherwise be. They motivate us to reach deep within ourselves and make our homes, our communities and our country somehow better. Barack Obama has a charismatic quality that does indeed mesmerize crowds

and make them cheer, but effective oratory can mislead, manipulate, and produce nothing.

Barack Obama's narrow views, fueled by his own individualistic and political aspirations, have forced him to promote objectives that are contrary to our faith and our belief system as Black Americans. His agenda actually demands we forsake our moral center and set aside what God has laid before us as our foundation for a productive and fulfilling life.

Barack Obama's positions on several issues are directly opposed to Black America's interests in cultivating a better life for our people and humanity.

Abortion

Planned Parenthood, one of the leading special interest groups supporting Barack Obama, has a racist history that would cause any American, Black or White, to recoil. Founded originally by Margaret Sanger, it was a means of curtailing Black births in America. Many in the Black American community simply call it what it is: *genocide.*

> **Barack Obama's positions on several issues are directly opposed to Black America's interests...**

According to Sanger, "When motherhood becomes the fruit of a deep yearning, not the result of ignorance or accident, its children will become the foundation of a new race."

Barack Obama spoke these words in an address before the Planned Parenthood Action Fund (PPAF) in July 2007:

"There will always be people, many of goodwill, who do not share my view on the issue of choice. On this fundamental issue, I will not yield and Planned Parenthood will not yield."

It is beyond comprehension how someone who touts himself as a "Black American" cannot only take money from, but overtly support an organization that sought to systemically eliminate our entire race from existence in the United States. So much for humanity.

Consider these opposing views expressed by Dr. Alveda King:

"Planned Parenthood is no stranger to deception. I know first-hand because prior to my abortion, a Planned Parenthood doctor told me that my baby was just a 'blob of tissue." Now, Planned Parenthood lies by trying to imply that my uncle, Dr. Martin Luther King, Jr., would somehow endorse the organization today. He most certainly would not.

"Uncle Martin accepted an award from Planned Parenthood in 1966 when abortion was illegal in every state and before Planned Parenthood started publicly advocating for it. In Planned Parenthood's own citation for Uncle Martin's prize, not only is no mention of abortion made, it states that 'human life and progress are indeed indivisible.' In 1966, neither the general public nor my uncle was aware of the true agenda of Planned Parenthood, an agenda of death that has become painfully obvious as the years have unfolded."

Dr. King said, "The Negro cannot win if he is willing to sacrifice the future of his children for personal comfort and safety,' and, 'Injustice anywhere is a threat to injustice everywhere.' There is no way he would want his name or image associated today with Planned Parenthood, the group most responsible for denying civil rights to the over 45 million American babies killed by abortion, one-third of them African-American."

Gay Marriage

As a Christian of deep faith and belief in what the Scriptures tell us, I cannot justify erasing 2,000 years of human history that has defined marriage as a union between a man and a woman. It goes against our Black American foundation.

Gay relationships are not about procreation. They are about one's sexual preference. Extending "rights" based on one's sexual preference is nothing more than seeking society's blessing for your behavior. *The gay agenda is in no way comparable to the Civil Rights Movement.* To suggest this, as some have, including Barack Obama, is deeply offensive to me as a Black American.

If gay marriage becomes legal throughout the United States, the results will weaken Black American families at a time when they need all the nurturing and support we can give them. Study after study shows that children reared with *both a mother and a father* are less likely to use drugs, engage in premarital sex, live in poverty, drop out of school or commit suicide. Gay marriage will only worsen the plight of Black Americans and Americans in general. Again, so much for the broader concerns of humanity.

Burdening Working People With Ever Higher Taxes

To feed the ravenous appetite of an ever-expanding federal government, Barack Obama needs one thing—your money. He gains greater power and influence from using your tax dollars to reward special interest groups for their support, and creating more government programs to secure your dependency and votes.

How humane is it strip a person of their dignity and pride, by basically telling them they will never amount to anything without the federal government's help? How humane is it to *so tightly* lock a segment of the population into a downward spiral of government dependency, that they have no hope of ever experiencing a sense of accomplishment and achievement—something inherent in the human soul?

As stated in Chapter One, Obama's tax-raising plan is not meant to help the middle class and struggling Black Americans; it is meant to reward special interests, punish entrepreneurs, and create more government dependency.

How does this make us better people? In America, we have a long tradition of philanthropy unmatched by any other nation in the world. We are undoubtedly generous. Is paying more of our hard earned dollars to bureaucrats in Washington a prescription for encouraging our people to work hard and do more for those in need? No. When I keep more of the money I earn I am better able to take care of my family, tithe to my church, and donate my time and money to help those who need it. Again, that is part of my Black American foundation.

> **Obama's tax-raising plan is not meant to help the middle class and struggling Black Americans...**

At the very least taxing away more of our hard earned money does not inspire us to greatness—it promotes mediocrity. Once more, so much for the broader concerns of humanity, Mr. Obama.

Dr. King: "Change does not roll in on the wheels of inevitability, but comes through continuous struggle. And so we must straighten our backs and work for our freedom. A man can't ride you unless your back is bent."

These stirring words send a surge of courage through my bones every time I read them – and summarize why I am standing up and speaking out against Barack Obama.

It makes me cry out, "How dare he!" Given the crowds of fawning worshippers at his political rallies, it seems many Black Americans are ready to bend their backs and let Barack Obama ride on them into office. He and the mainstream media have deemed his victory inevitable on the false premise that he, too, has experienced our continuous struggle as a Black American. He is neither inevitable, (or anointed in my book), nor has any concept of the foundation on which Black Americans have endured their struggle throughout history.

The change Obama advocates is one where you and I remain complacent while he implements an agenda that will do one thing—bend our lives to the will of the government. Bend our lives and our backs, so Barack Obama can ride on to victory.

Barack Obama clearly favors a Communist approach to governing. Knowing the failed history of Communism, is this the correct path to innovation, growth and opportunity for Black America and all our citizens? Wouldn't you much rather straighten your back and work for your own prosperity knowing that ultimately, this is what results in strong families and a strong nation?

Barack Obama's proposed agenda for expanding more government control over every aspect our lives is leading our country more and more away from the core principles of responsibility, faith, hard work and strong families that has made our nation the greatest place on earth. Never forget this truth about government: the more it gives, the more it takes!

The more you and I depend on government, the less freedom we have. How dare we, as Americans—no matter our ethnicity—bend our backs and just let Barack Obama ride into the sunset with our freedoms in tow! There is nothing better for America and the world than a free people, self-reliant, unfettered by government, and living and working under their own direction, according to their own definition of success. That is not only God's plan; as Americans, it is our destiny.

Let us straighten our backs and accept that preserving freedom requires our diligence—and sometimes sacrifice. We must look inside ourselves yet again and find the strength to throw off the oppressor. We must do this if we are to keep all that we have won for the generations to come.

Dr. King: "Every man must decide whether he will walk in the light of creative altruism or in the darkness of destructive selfishness."
Many Black Americans —and I count myself among them—fear Barack Obama's message is leading us into darkness. To me, what Dr. King meant by creative altruism was summoning the innate goodness that lies within each of us to help one another. This is nothing more or less than the essence of our Christian faith. Christ did not say, "Let Rome help people." Dr. King's message was not about government doing the heavy lifting; it was about human beings helping those in need – and thereby finding God in the process.

When Dr. King warned of the darkness of destructive selfishness, I truly believe he meant abdicating our responsibilities as citizens. As God fearing people, allowing the government to take over our responsibilities gives us the easy way out and we suffer the consequences as a people and as a nation. How does the federal government improve us as human beings? How are our spirits enriched and our souls fed when we relinquish our duties to one another to a bloated bureaucracy?

My friends, it doesn't. Incrementally, religion and God were banished in the Soviet Union and the Communist bloc. The playbook was simple. First you give up your faith in God, and then you place your faith in government. There you have it: the lie, the manipulation, the slippery slope which allowed millions of people in Eastern Europe to plunge into poverty, starvation and death. Barack Obama and the liberals in his party religiously adhere to this playbook under the guise of creative altruism, masking their destructive selfishness.

Every man must decide for himself whether he will walk in light or darkness. I choose the light. I reject the destructive selfishness of government-sanctioned altruism as espoused by Barack Obama.

Barack Obama cannot hold a candle to the clear pure light of inspired thought from Dr. Martin Luther King, Jr. Dr. King had a dream of an America where individuals could experience the realities of their full potential by the content of their character. Obama has a dream, but it does not benefit Black America, only himself and the elitist few.

At some point, right-thinking men and women must listen to their still small voice and say, "Enough."

CHAPTER FOUR

Hope and Change: It's Already Ours

I remember hearing a story on the radio some time ago I would like to share.

One morning, while a man was enjoying his usual cup of coffee, he noticed birds picking up the crumbs of fresh bread and muffins being tossed to them by people sitting at tables around him.

He decided to try a little experiment. Clearly these birds expected their daily ration of crumbs, so the next day he arrived a bit early and placed an object within the area where patrons normally tossed crumbs for the birds. He sat patiently, but no birds came. When other customers arrived and started tossing out crumbs, the birds immediately flew in and perched upon the object he had earlier placed within their reach, waiting for more crumbs.

As people began to leave and the crumb-tossing ceased, the birds departed. He reached down and picked up the object he had brought for them to enjoy. It was a loaf of bread. A small lesson, to be sure, but a valuable one. The birds were fixed on the easy route — waiting for crumbs to be tossed to them. All the while they were sitting on a mother lode of food, but would not take the time to work and unlock its greater riches.

Is this not representative of the human condition? All of us—no matter our ethnicity—prefer the easy route. Unfortunately, in this day and age we seem to be almost addicted to the easy route, and for what? Crumbs...

The other day while I was watching C-SPAN, a Black American woman verbally attacked Presidential candidate, John McCain, with tough questions about what he intended to do about her daily plight once in office. Her request was basically a laundry list of, "what are you going to do about low income housing, job training for our teenagers and resources for our unemployment situation?" In fact, her position was primarily, "how do you intend to take care of me?"

The entire time I watched this exchange I was struck by one simple fact. The woman's premise was that John McCain and the federal government should provide all solutions and benefits for the American people. In other words, offer her more crumbs.

I shook my head. This woman's entire line of questioning assumed that whatever the problem was, it could only be solved by our government. As a confident and discerning Black American citizen of our republic, do YOU really believe this? Do you accept her premise? I sincerely hope not.

> **You need to understand that, as an American citizen, you are sitting on a loaf of bread**

This woman approaches problems from the perspective that someone else—in this case the government—should do for her rather than her doing for herself; and what she is demanding government to do, quite frankly, is perverse. It is contrary to human nature and what God has set before us as our foundation: faith in Him and ourselves.

If this woman stopped just sitting on her loaf of bread, she could tap into her own God-given talent, ability, and competitive nature, and would be surprised at the opportunity that lies within her reach. But, when you have a "crumb mentality" you begin to fuss at the people who are giving you the crumbs, feeling somehow you deserve bigger portions. After all, you've been coming to this table for years and it's time for an increase! Right? Wrong! You need to understand that, as an American citizen, you are sitting on a loaf of bread...a big one.

Who dispenses the crumbs? The government, of course. Candidates like Barack Obama utilize the "crumb mentality" to further their ridiculous grab for power and the dominance it gives them over us as a people. Does this advance our freedom as Black Americans? No. Too many of us are left perching atop a loaf of bread, sacrificing our votes and opportunities for more crumbs. *It is way past time for Black Americans to take inventory of their self-worth and their ability to compete without waiting for the crumbs to be handed to them.*

Let me be candid. Affirmative Action could never give me what I am truly worth, and we simply cannot afford to build the next generation's success off of it. Once upon a time, Affirmative Action may have helped level the playing field, and perhaps it was necessary to do this. I have no doubt those that implemented this policy had honorable intentions. However, has not this day passed?

Affirmative Action carries a risk. If we are not careful, we will be perceived as somehow less qualified—just another dependent little bird sitting on a loaf of bread waiting for another crumb, but this time with a couple of almonds tossed in. *Black Americans must identify themselves as successful in their own right if they expect others to perceive them in this way.* Admit it. Do you not feel in your heart of hearts that we as Black Americans have allowed the mainstream media, with the help of liberal politicians, to continually portray the Black American as a dismal and frustrated people?

We, as a people, are worth far more than crumbs and almonds. Look at your legacy and foundation as a Black American. Your strength, your self-worth, your fulfillment comes from within. I believe in my heart God made it this way. Success in life is all about how you choose to see yourself, mixed in with a healthy dose of faith, family, hard work and a will that says, "I will never give up."

Real hope and change does not come from a salesman, a charlatan, like Barack Obama and his vision of an ever-expanding federal government dispensing crumbs. Obama and today's so-called Black leaders, who have been handed the "keys" to our voices, can only sell the empty promise of hope and change to a people who are unsure of themselves. If you are not careful, their lethal prescription for your life will result in dignity being sucked from your soul, courage wrenched from your heart, and opportunity from your grasp. And for what? Crumbs…

Moses My Servant is Dead

Moses my servant is dead, God told Joshua. It's well past time for the Joshuas of our generation to take their rightful place and speak with a different voice – one that is confident, free, and positive. One that sees our collective glass as half full, not half empty. A voice that proclaims we are incredibly competent, creative, patriotic, God-fearing people, who are fully capable of contributing on every level of our society.

I would urge us all as Black Americans to turn away from the grousing, frowning "Black leaders" who have their own political agenda. Do you really want their negative thinking clouding your mind and poisoning your positive vision for your life? Seriously question the motivations of manipulating politicians like Barack Obama. Do you really believe Barack Obama and Big Government can solve your problems in life?

I choose to embrace a better way of thinking.

Let us turn to our common foundation as Black Americans: faith, family and hard work, and embrace it fully. Let us make a commitment to one another as Black Americans to ramp up all we are doing to emphasize education, create new businesses, and expand the ones we have.

Let us choose to see a big loaf of bread that represents the great American dream and work to secure a nice slice of it. Our capitalistic system is the envy of the world and it is our unbridled entrepreneurship that affords us innovation and economic strength. As Black Americans, let us reach out and do business with the world, not because we feel we deserve it, but because we have the inherent right and ability to do so. Contrast this with the candidate, Barack Obama. His emphasis on big government as our savior is naïve if he believes it, and the worst sort of pandering for Black American votes if he does not. Just like any other American, let's compete in the marketplace. My philosophy is simply this—this is America and we are Americans. As Black Americans, we can achieve anything we set our hearts and minds to do under the umbrella of freedom our nation provides.

I cannot tell you how many times I have heard the word "no." Ask any successful person and they will say the same. I've never talked to a successful person who has not had to overcome adversity, and yet persevered to finally achieve their goal. Eventually somebody will say "yes." Once you give them the very best you've got, you will build trust and with that trust comes loyalty.

Inner-city Asian Americans offer an interesting example. They open their small businesses and work hard while maintaining strong families. They are prudent and thrifty. As a result they enjoy stability, independence, and economic prosperity. They don't ask anyone to do business with them; they allow anyone and everyone to choose their service. We gladly eat in their restaurants and take our clothes to their cleaning establishments. If it's good we come back, if it's not, we don't and we tell others to avoid that business. This is how things work. Good service, good quality, and good price almost always wins.

My purpose is not to present a small business primer, but rather to point out what makes someone successful in business and in life. It is not rocket science.

The Perception of Black America

In our media saturated culture, perception is everything. We must work together to change how our society views Black Americans, and we should start with the media, which includes Hollywood.

For years the media has distorted who and what we are as Black Americans, and, when viewed as a whole, it is not a positive image. More often than not we are represented as dishonest, immoral and violent. When was the last time you saw, on a sustained basis, the presentation of the Black American in a positive way? Most of us work hard, go to church, and love and nurture our families. We love our country and want to preserve and protect and improve it. Black Americans have and continue to make important contributions to our society at all levels.

The on-going barrage of negative impressions—in the news and the entertainment industry—is simply not a realistic portrayal of Black Americans. More disturbing is the bigger and bigger toll the negative portrayal of Black Americans is taking on us!

We're classified as men who rap, murder and avoid being husbands to our wives and fathers to our children. Sure we know it's not true, but the media is not interested in what we know; they are interested in ratings and keeping us believing that what they are reporting is the truth. The primary toll is how it is causing us to see ourselves, and if we are beginning to believe it.

A positive and more realistic portrayal of Black Americans would result in a tremendous shift in how we see ourselves and would only enhance our journey into the 21st Century.

Recently I had a discussion with a close friend about this and he hit the nail on the head when he reflected on the response to the verdict of the O.J. Simpson case years ago.

The Black community was elated when Simpson was declared not guilty of murder. Living rooms erupted with screams; barbershops and beauty salons were filled with people throwing high-fives. Simpson's guilt or innocence was not the issue in their minds. The fact that Simpson beat the charges in a perceived White court of law was the core issue. It gave Black Americans a sense of vindication. After all, these were the same courts that put many of our sons in prison.

Was it good for Black Americans to be seen by society as being more concerned with O.J. Simpson beating the system than the charge of murdering two fellow human beings in cold blood, particularly when the body of evidence *could have* pointed to his guilt? This was the concern my friend was raising, which I believe is valid. You and I must consider the implications if we are to be honest.

> You and I must consider the implications if we are to be honest.

The prospect of Barack Obama being the first Black American President brings the same kind of elation. A rush of euphoria. I caution us all to stop, take a breath and consider whether or not we really want to place our faith and trust in someone we do not know. Are we once again, as with the Simpson trial, potentially allowing vindication to trump truth? Especially for a man who presents himself as a Black American but who actually is not? A man who espouses positions, like Simpson, which are clearly contrary to our Black American foundation?

Barack Obama may be one expensive ride we simply cannot afford to take. There are many well-meaning Black Americans who expect much from this man based on hollow promises. No politician, no government, can ever deliver this much. I'm reminded of a pop song from years ago, *I Can't Get No Satisfaction*. Barack Obama wants your Black American vote—but he will never give you *satisfaction*.

It's Yours Already

There is one irrefutable truth about poverty that many refuse to accept: It will always be with us.

It's impossible to do away with poverty simply because it's impossible to control what people do and what they choose to believe. For Barack Obama to suggest—as he continually does—that he can wave a magic wand and do away with the natural consequences of people's choices in life is to play God. No politician can deliver on this promise. Barack Obama asks you to believe that he can. Barack as your savior? Truth or lie? Listen to that still small voice.

Put aside Barack Obama's skin color, as this is not the O.J. Simpson trial, it is the election of the next President of the United States. Look deeper and tell me what you really see. I see a person who is not honest about who he is or what he intends to do as President. This makes me unsure, and afraid. Yes, I am afraid of Barack Obama. An honest man does not continually make promises he cannot keep— like righting all the wrongs done to our people through legislation and bigger government. Do you really believe this is possible? I for one do not. It's a way of buying votes.

What do I mean when I say, "It's yours already"? I mean there is no need for us as Black Americans to vote for a pandering politician like Barack Obama who promises things he cannot deliver to get our votes. The things you and I need are, in truth, ours already. If you want to start a business…get on with it. If you want to improve your marriage…change your behavior. If you want to get an education…there is a library in your town or city and tuition loans available. If you want to travel the world…you can do it by saving the money or getting a job that takes you far and wide.

Sure these things present challenges you must overcome. But so what? Toughen up. Compete. Set your goals and stick to them. In the words of Edna in one of my children's favorite animated movies, *The Incredibles*, "Go—Fight—Win!" The means and the ability to have what you want in life lies within yourself. None of this is Barack Obama's to hand out like candy to little kids. It's all about you. It's all about building your life on the Black American foundation that is yours by right and the grace of God.

Think Truth, Not Color

There is not a person on this planet that has not been affected by the warped minds of people who think they are better than others. Black people in particular, have been singled out and discriminated against because of this mindset. We must resist any limitations other people try to impose on us as Black Americans. We cannot allow other people to determine our self-worth. Think of it this way. You can tie a small rope around an elephant's foot when it is a baby to restrict its movement. From then on – even when the elephant has matured to a five ton giant – it will still remain tethered in place by that small rope it could easily flick off.

We cannot let other people tether us through psychological manipulation, or hold us back with media propaganda that causes us to somehow believe we are less worthy. We control our own destiny. Barack Obama and those in his party certainly do not—and they never will.

One reason I often reference our Constitution and Bill of Rights is because those who drafted this document advanced a radical idea in the time in which they lived. They pledged their lives, their liberty and their sacred honor in support of it. That once radical idea is this: All men are created equal and possess the God-given the right to be free and pursue their own vision of happiness. It has been a long, painful road in our country, but it is our objective to realize our full potential as Black Americans and citizens of this nation that is our home.

Race cannot be the reason why Black Americans vote for Barack Obama, or any candidate. Do not equate a man of color occupying the highest office in the land with your freedom. You are already free. Perhaps you are like the baby elephant. The little rope in your mind is holding you back. Break free from that rope. Do not permit the media and the manipulative voices of others bind you and prevent you from seeing what is the truth and what is a lie.

Every individual has the freedom and the ability to think of himself or herself in the larger arena of where they live, not just in terms of their race. Certainly I am not suggesting we can easily ignore injustices of the past or of the present. There is a lot of it, to be sure. What I am saying is let's take a different track and rethink what is working and what is not.

As Black Americans, let us rethink our own handling of racial issues right in our own homes and in our own communities. In essence, what exactly are you and I doing with what we already have?

• Are we being faithful husbands, fathers, wives and mothers?

• Are we creating an environment and setting a standard whereby our children can excel academically?

• Are we holding to a standard of morality that, by our example, will ensure our children a future that contains a sound family life? As examples, are we offering our community and society gifts and talents that serve to make our country better?

•Are we involving ourselves in the political debate, running for office, and attempting to change legislation that would benefit everyone—not just Blacks, but all Americans?

•Are we teaching our children to study our history and love their country so they realize what freedoms we enjoy under our Constitution?

•Are we doing everything we can to prepare our children for leadership within the Black American political arena—to ensure that there is room at the table for us tomorrow?

It is past time for us to honestly and forthrightly confront the reality that there are detrimental things we as Black Americans have permitted to exist within our own communities. These things do far greater harm than someone calling us the "N" word. (Excuse me, but I still can't believe we are even talking about a word.)

• We are the ones who permit our daughters to become involved in sexual promiscuity.

• We are the ones who allow our sons to sow their wild oats and then shirk their responsibilities.

• We are the ones who tolerate poor examples to be celebrated by our youth because of their popularity as a recording artist or television celebrity.

• We are the ones who place more emphasis on the shoes we put on our feet than the knowledge we put in our heads.

• We are the ones who buy the biggest automobiles and houses in order to feel like we have arrived.

I could go on and on pointing out the double standards that exist within our own lives as Black Americans. But let me get this off my chest. It is hypocritical to judge what a person is doing against you, when you refuse to take responsibility for what you are, in effect, doing to yourself.

I'll be the first to tell you that I cannot begin to understand all the pain that my ancestors went through. Nor do I in any way excuse those persons who did it to them. I have not studied Black history to the extent that I have documented the grinding oppression and horrible lynchings that were perpetrated against innocent Black people down through the years.

No reasonable person of any color can excuse or ignore this.

What I can say is that White people are not responsible for our people allowing *our* sons to impregnate *our* daughters, and send them to the abortion clinic to not create another problem.

Yes, racism has been an ugly blight on our society. A part of our shared past that fills any thinking person with a feeling of sadness and regret—and for those that choose to embrace it, *anger.* In truth, some minds will never be changed when it comes to people of other races. But I choose to walk on the bright side of the road. Let's turn our collective cheek, break free of that rope and embrace our freedom.

Black President or White President. Food stamps or no food stamps. Affirmative Action, or no Affirmative Action. Whatever the self-appointed Black American, Barack Obama, promises to get your vote, it does not matter when you rely on our foundation. God has doors He will open for you that no man can close. I am convinced of this. For every time you are told "no" because you are Black, White, fat, skinny, young or old, God has four people waiting who will tell you, "You're just the person we're looking for!"

Stop Taking Your Blackness So Seriously

When, as Black Americans, we want to make sure people treat us right, we are, in essence, subjugating ourselves to those very people.

Not long ago I found myself watching a television program where a panel of Black Americans discussed race and equality. I listened for a while and then turned to my wife and said, "This conversation has not changed one bit after all these years. Where is the progress?" To see high profile and distinguished Black American guests participating in this conversation was equally disturbing.

These "distinguished" guests merely tossed the same old clichés back and forth, and simply bickered amongst themselves. In disgust, I turned off the television and sat there frustrated. If a truly racist person had been part of that panel discussion, they could not have done a better job than these Black participants in talking down Black Americans. Instead of discussing real solutions for racial equality, they only perpetuated a false and negative perception of who we are as a people.

> **As Black Americans are we hurting ourselves by being too focused on race?**

As Black Americans are we hurting ourselves by being too focused on race?

Let us look at ourselves as Black Americans and ask why people treat us in a certain way. I honestly feel it is mostly because we have made our blackness too big of a deal. We create an atmosphere for racial division when we arrive with our arms folded and with a presumed attitude that someone is going to be unfair. I love setting the atmosphere wherever I go. It is amazing how people expect me to be "Black" rather than just another human being who happens to be

Black. Letting people get to know who you are as a person, is just as important as you getting to know who that other person really is. I truly believe God is with His children on this issue. Love wins out every time. Hate is poison and the losing hand.

Racism exists not because people don't like each other; it exists and continues on because we simply do not understand one another. Most Black Americans who excessively fuss about racism have not attempted to have a sincere conversation with a White person. They are somehow conditioned to focus solely on what the person across from them looks like. Conversely, White Americans are equally guilty of making the same judgment. We only see the skin color.

My counsel is to quit taking your skin color so seriously and just live. You may be thinking about your color while the other person isn't giving it any thought. With 300 million people in America, you cannot tell me you will only find a few people who are different from you and still like you for who you are. You may be hanging around the wrong folks and believing the wrong story. You will never soar with eagles if you are angrily sitting on that loaf of bread picking up crumbs. It's your life. Clear your head and get on with it. You don't need a fake Black American like Barack Obama to validate who you are.

I remember being pulled over by a cop years ago for making a quick left turn that almost resulted in an accident. I was in the hood in Oakland, California returning home from a basketball game when I remembered I had left my driver's license behind. I took a quick left to turn around and two White cops were right on me. I placed my hands on the steering wheel of my beat up white Ford LTD II as the policemen approached the car.

I said, "Hello, officers. How are you? Sorry about that left turn. Believe it or not I was turning around to get my driver's license that I left in my friend's car at the park." The one officer said, "So you don't have your license?" I replied, "No sir, I don't." He proceeded to get my name and social security number and then handcuffed me and put me in the back seat of the patrol car. After asking me a few questions, he inquired about what was in my trunk.

It occurred to me that I had some books I had written in the trunk. The cops retrieved one of my books and began to read it. One of them asked me to finish a line that he had started to read aloud, and I did. They let me go. Upon leaving one officer said, "Get out of here before I put this pencil up your nose." "Yes, sir," I replied.

Basically, I refused to respond as if they were going to treat me as a Black male in the hood with no driver's license. Instead, I elected to treat them with respect and did not make my color an issue. As a result, I controlled the outcome more than they did. I remained optimistic that everything would work out. At one point, they actually started laughing at my attempt to put them at ease. They assumed I was going to be a problem.

My genuineness came across to their human side and it all worked out. I could have snapped back when he told me that he would stick his pencil up my nose, but I cut him a break because my words would have been too heavy for him anyway. I think he was more upset that I did not give him an excuse to treat me as a Black male than just a person who forgot his driver's license. I defused the situation using reason.

I personally have never had a problem with White people. That doesn't mean they haven't had some problem with me, however. I have often pondered this. My conclusion? I think it may be because I do not expect to have a problem. If I sense a White person has a problem with me, I simply don't feed it my attention. After all, that person doesn't really know who I am anyway. Why should I allow his or her problem to become my problem? I have better things to do. Such people are "kryptonite" and I am superman. I do not let them weaken my spirit much less spoil my day. As a result, I'm not delayed from reaching my goals. There are more ways to reach my goals than through one negative, fear-ridden person. Besides, I believe more people want to help me than hurt me, and those are the kinds of people I attract and hang around regardless of skin color.

I sometimes think younger generations do not have my—and perhaps your—frame of reference. I would love to safely conduct an experiment I believe would be very revealing. It goes something like this: place five White men and five Black men, along with their wives, alone the remote Kodiak Island off the coast of Alaska. Give them enough water and food for a week but no weapons to protect themselves.

Kodiak Island is home to the Kodiak bear, the largest carnivore on earth. I guarantee all of these men will look past their skin color and realize their survival is directly linked to one another. They will quickly become "brothers." It's them or the bears. After a week passes and they have been picked up, I bet they will celebrate with a feast and likely remain lifelong friends, family even, because of their shared experience and the adversity they overcame together.

Ask any Marine, any Navy Seal, any soldier in the Army or airman in the Air Force. They will tell you who their real brothers are. For the combat soldier, it has nothing to do with skin color. It's duty, honor and country. It's content of character all the way. And, my fellow Black American, who said that best? It was certainly not Barack Obama.

We have all seen White people take their anger out on Black Americans. Some still think they are better than we are. They live in the past. They drive by and gun their engines as if this is going to somehow make their lives better. It pains me. I realize many people have lost jobs because Affirmative Action laws have extended preference to

Black Americans. It is the law of unintended consequences. Affirmative Action, at one time, may have had a worthwhile objective, but it is time we compute the price and see if the return is worth it. *When you legislate to achieve a benefit for one group, you often create resentment and bitterness in the hearts and minds of another.*

Voting for Barack Obama because we think he is one of us and will somehow bring "hope" and "change" is a pitiful excuse and the easy way out from under our own lack of responsibility in facing our own internal issues. If we are not willing to hold our own Black leaders and ourselves accountable, then how dare we assume that putting a self-appointed Black American in office will make our lives better? Moreover, will Barack Obama further perpetuate the false and negative perceptions of Black Americans? Will he actually create more racial disharmony?

I've been thinking about this.

If I had only five minutes with Barack Obama what would I say to him? I think it would go something like this: "Mr. Obama, tax us fairly, give us no favors and just protect our freedoms and we will do the rest."

If I could address the House of Representatives in full session what would I say? I would start off my speech with a ringing declaration: "Just assure us of our freedoms and leave our Bill of Rights and the Constitution alone. Stop fussing, and fire some of those special interest lawyers who use up most of the resources that we need. We'll make it. We've come this far as a people and as a nation and we will make it."

Believe With Me

I believe the best days for Black Americans are right before them
I believe the power of change lies within them
I believe the will to achieve is deeper
than the judgments about them

I now know that my belief is justified
When I see the places we have arrived
Despite the hindrances of others

I believe the best days for Black Americans are right before them
I believe the power of change lies within them
I believe the will to achieve is deeper
than the judgments about them

Look up—I know you see it too
Refuse the news that's old and those that refuse to grow
Turn to the God who has made you and placed
within you treasures untold
Reach for them, touch them, and live it beautifully for all to see

I believe the best days for Black Americans are right before them
I believe the power of change lies within them
I believe the will to achieve is deeper
than the judgments about them

I believe.
Believe with me.

William G. Owens © 2008

CHAPTER FIVE

AMERICA FROM A BLACK
FAMILY'S PERSPECTIVE

A Father's Perspective
by William Owens

As a father, my interest lies in ensuring that my family has the freedoms necessary to fulfill their dreams. This involves the empowerment to choose men and women who will rule according to a higher standard of life, not a standard of the people. When we vote, we should do so with a confidence that they administrate with a principle that holds America to a steady hand to navigate the uncertain seas of adversity and adversaries. This cannot be done in a glass house of philosophies that presumes hope and change will come by sheer force of will. It must be communicated to my family that such a candidate has a well thought out plan that is based on hope but rooted in reality.

As a Christian, I don't believe that a potential presidential candidate has to share my beliefs. I respect the beliefs of my neighbors as well as my President's. Should Obama be elected, I would do all that is in my ability to support him for the good of this nation as long as it does not contradict my core beliefs of life, liberty and the pursuit of happiness. There are countless policies that would appear to be good when you look at them at surface value. As fathers, we must look deeper. It's our role to protect and to provide for our families; and the first line of defense is ensuring that we have a father (or mother) in the White House who is sensitive to our role as parents.

Parenting styles are as different as our upbringings. Some of us were disciplined differently than others. One child was told to go stand in the corner; another was told to get his or her britches down. One was intellectually persuaded to be obedient; the other was told to obey or else. Others had a combination of both. Children from all sides of experiences have either turned progressed or digressed.

Can you really trace an adult's current state of life back to whether or not the parent did everything right? I'm not a psychologist; I simply believe that each individual is capable of choosing their quality of life regardless of the conflict he or she had or did not have as a child. Of course, there are extreme cases where it is difficult to get on with daily life without drawing from our past. The difference is some build on their past in a positive way, while others build on their past a negative way. The choice, whether fair or not, is always the builder, not the material.

What's my point? Black Americans must not entrust the "hope" and "courage" of Obama without the substance to back it up. Nor should we do so for any candidate. You might ask, "Why aren't you writing a book about McCain?" As Black Americans, we already look at McCain for what he stands for; when we see Obama, we are assumptive because he looks like us. *Why Black America Should Have Doubts* means just that. The doubt is based on both sides:

> The difference is some build on their past in a positive way, while others build on their past a negative way.

Obama's patched-up and many times contradictions of policy and motive versus our raising our fist and saying, "Give the brother a chance!"

As a father, an important element of Obama's motives is the fact that he does not have a viable history of his father for me to relate to. Relate to doesn't mean I need to read a heavy volume of his personal history. It is important, however, for me, as a father, to have a sense of my President's life with his father perhaps because he, himself, was never validated as a son from his father. I mean no disrespect, however, we cannot ignore what this could imply seeing the extreme lack of fathers within Black American communities.

We all, on a subconscious level, are trying to find out what makes people "tick." It's common language within the Black community to hear someone say, "He/she has issues" or even hear ourselves say, "Child, leave me alone. I got issues." Every American has cause to be concerned about the stability of one's mindset and when we analyze just some of Obama's speeches and his book.

As a Black American son and father, my father always affirms me by the smallest of things. Talking on the phone, laughing over a something that took place years ago or even just thinking about him. This is so critically important; it keeps me grounded. I'm also involved in many aspects of my children's life, as much as they permit me to be, seeing them growing and become more independent by the day. I'll be the first to tell you that Selena and I have an awesome relationship with our children and sometimes, as any parents, we have our moments as well. The presence of family is never compromised, no matter how difficult or how distant we might be. Nothing my children could ever do or become would cease my love for them; and I feel that same way about my parents. It provides us as children (of which we always are to our parents) a sense of value, which in turn causes us to value others in our judgment and decision making process as adults.

A final thought to Black fathers. Understand that your ability to father your children, love your wife and be of value to your community is more important than who is President of the United States. Whoever you vote for President of the United States will make your role as father and husband easier or more difficult. I pray you look beyond the skin.

The Breakdown of the Family Unit
Under an Obama Presidency

By Selena Owens

Note to Readers: I am a woman of mixed ethnicity. I feel it is important to say this upfront because so many people have questions: Is she Black? Is she part White? If she's not Black, then why is she speaking out on Black issues? I'm not trying to defend my position as to why I can relate to the issues detailed in this book; I am simply attempting to answer the natural tendency of people to inquire about my ethnicity. I was birthed into this world from parents of mixed heritage: Puerto Rican, Portuguese and other ethnicities that got into the mix via my parents. My father's people hail from the Madeira Islands of Portugal, near the tip of North Africa. My mother's people are primarily Spanish and of other European descent. I grew up in the tenement housing projects in a village in New York with friends of all ethnicities. Basically, everyone who was poor lived where we lived no matter his or her ethnicity.

It's no secret that the Black heritage runs in our family. All of my siblings and I have spouses or significant others who are Black. I don't think it ever really crossed our minds to consider otherwise. It was a natural inclination to gravitate to Black persons or people of color.

Although I don't readily encounter as much discrimination in society as I've seen happen to Black Americans, it is nonetheless there. I've experienced it in places such as contemporary churches, home school centers, wellness centers and other places that are primarily populated by White families, (especially when they lay eyes on my husband.) To be fair, I've encountered prejudice from Black individuals because I'm not fully Black or don't share the same "Black" interests. Or because I don't sound "Black." Whatever that means.

I believe that if a person wants to find fault with another human being, he or she will. I do not apologize for who I am, what I have or have not experienced, or what my interests are. I am who God created me to be and my purpose in life is to love my family and contribute wherever and whatever I can to society.

I also do not apologize for believing that a Barack Obama Presidency will have a detrimental affect on Black American families.

Moral Decay in Our Land

Let's face it. America has lost its moral compass. Over the years, this country has witnessed a moral corrosion of epic proportion: gay marriage vs. traditional marriage; same-sex prom king and queen events; record numbers of STD's among teens, Internet predators, middle school children "deciding" to become another sex; and the outright assault on Christianity in the name of religious tolerance. Each day we witness more and more perverse and distressing headlines regarding the moral decay of our nation.

Have Americans gone to sleep? What have we been viewing on television? What's been going on in our daily lives? Have we just buried our heads in the sand and laid down our weapons and allowed the assault to happen? These issues are plaguing families, confusing children, and threatening our parental rights.

In this explosive information age, our children are being blasted with negative messages on television, in the movies, on the Internet, on the cell phone and on the iPod. Parents, already struggling to rear their children, are now faced with a multi-faceted assault on the morals and values they are attempting to instill in their children.

It is no secret the affect Hollywood and celebrity have on our youth. "Celebrity worship now provides and important reference point for growing up. It is part of the transfer of attachment from parents to peer group. Also, whereas in past times family, friends and teachers were influential role models, celebrities now fulfill that role," says John Maltby, a professor at Leicester University. Mr. Maltby co-authored a study on youth attitudes toward celebrities.

The very same celebrities, who believe they have so much influence over the political process, shirk the responsibility of the influence they *do have* on our youth. Why would Barack Obama, who is so quick to parade his family in front of the cameras, be so closely tied to the very people who tell our girls to put their brains in their purses and our boys that men are either bumbling idiots or abusers?

According to Barack Obama:

"It's up to us—as fathers and parents—to instill this ethic of excellence in our children. It's up to us to say to our daughters, don't ever let images on TV tell you what you are worth, because I expect you dream without limit and reach for those goal. It's up to us to tell our sons, those songs on the radio may glorify violence, but in my house we live glory to achievement, self respect and hard work."

If this is Obama's opinion, why in the world he is aligning himself with Hollywood, taking their campaign contributions, attending their fundraisers and accepting their endorsements?

Barack Obama is not only aligning himself with these celebrities in Hollywood, he is smugly becoming one. The rock star status he enjoys and uses to his benefit, further tells our youth stardom trumps substance. Why would he unite with the very people who have made our jobs as parents very difficult? Perhaps Mr. Obama, like the majority of the left in this country, believes parents are the problem and government is the solution.

Solutions in Disguise

What Barack Obama is presenting to this nation as "solutions" for our country is distressing. The most liberal member of the United States Senate cannot hide his socialistic outlook on an assortment of matters this country faces, particularly with regards to the American family. These issues are addressed in various segments of this book to weigh on your conscience and stir your soul to action. I want to engage you on the key moral and societal issues that every parent, every American, needs to give pause to, deeply ponder, and then courageously vote against this election year.

Your Daughter, Her Body—None of Your Business

It's no secret that abortion is rampant in America, especially in the Black community where it's touted as birth control. Ever notice how conveniently situated Planned Parenthood clinics are to urban Black communities? They aren't isolated away from the impoverished, pregnant teen; they are defiantly situated within her reach.

What about the underage girl who opts for abortion and cannot secretly obtain one because of her age? A President Obama would more than likely enact a loophole for her.

While serving in the United States Senate, Obama voted against the Child Interstate Abortion Notification Act (S.403). This bill prohibits minors from being taken across state lines without parental consent to undergo an abortion.

Forty-five states require parental consent or notification in order for a minor to have an abortion. This bill also permits a parent to sue any adult who knowingly assisted the minor across state lines to obtain an abortion, unless it was to save the life of the minor. It also ensures that an incestuous father cannot sue under the Act, and can be prosecuted for transporting his daughter across state lines to obtain an abortion. The Act also imposes a fine and/or prison term of up to one year on the doctor who performs an abortion on an out-of-state minor, in violation of parental notification requirements in their home state. www.baptistpress.com/bpnews.asp?id=21657 - 68k

Senator Obama feels that a parent does not deserve the right to have any input or knowledge of the decision for his or her underage child to undergo an abortion. Yet, study after study has shown the psychological effects abortion has on a woman, particularly teens. Teens who have abortions are more likely to have problems in relationships, commit suicide and seek treatment at mental health hospitals than women who had abortions as adults.

Obama's solution: let the government and child make the decision and leave the parents out of it, only to pick up the pieces later. Even if you don't have a teenage child, this should alarm you. If Obama strips parental rights in this most private and sensitive matter between a parent and his or her child, he will be at liberty to do it other areas as well.

Imagine this scenario: a teenage girl becomes pregnant. Whether or not it was "by mistake" or "unintentional" is not this issue here. She's pregnant. Now imagine this is YOUR daughter. Your daughter is scared... *very scared*. She knows that she is in a very precarious situation where there is no easy solution. She talks to her friends about it and they agree that she's too young to have a baby. "It would ruin your life," they tell her. Furthermore, they infuse her with fear by saying, "Your mom and dad would absolutely KILL you for this! Are you kidding? You can't tell them!"

In desperation, she seeks the advice of an abortion clinic "counselor" or some other individual who is a proponent of a "woman's right to choose." The person tells her in no uncertain terms that she has absolute control over her body and she can do with it whatever *she* feels is the right thing to do.

"But I can't tell my parents and I'm too young to have an abortion. I'm just fourteen years old!"

"I understand that but you can have an abortion in another state that provides this service for minors without parental consent. IT'S THE LAW!"

No matter what expense, it's the law. Parents are left in the dark regarding their children's health and welfare, but, hey, it's the law. This is America, right? Land of the free, home of the brave? Life, liberty, and the pursuit of happiness? This situation sounds more like death, bondage, and perpetual heartache. Thank you very much, President Obama. Pat yourself on the back; you've just contributed to the traumatized state of an American family.

> **Parents are left in the dark regarding their children's health and welfare, but, hey, it's the law.**

Don't even think for a minute that a teenage girl faced with this decision would not go through with an abortion. Frantic, fearful and feeling an impending sense of doom, she will make the choice to do what she's been "counseled" to do.

The point isn't that a child would be so conniving; the point is that if Obama has his way, the Child Interstate Abortion Notification Act (S.403) would not become law, and an underage pregnant teenager would have the right to make this type of decision without her parents' knowledge and their parental right to intervene and counsel her.

What the President Says Makes an Impression

Does what the President say or do have a lasting impact on children, teens and young adults? Absolutely. When former President Bill Clinton finally admitted to having sexual relations with then intern Monica Lewinsky, thousands of American teenagers and young adults mirrored his position on oral sex as not being real sex. Kelly Boggs of the Baptist Press noted, "It was Clinton's escapades with Monica Lewinsky that made oral sex a household topic in 1998. There is no doubt that the popularity of the topic at the time, coupled with Clinton's insistence that he did not have sex with Lewinsky, helped to contribute to the attitudes of many of today's teenagers."
http://www.sbcbaptistpress.org/bpnews.asp?id=21657

On the lighter side, when former President George H.W. Bush declared to the White House chefs his strong disdain of broccoli, this tidbit traveled like lightning around the media. Overnight, primary and middle school children steadfastly declared to their parents, teachers and school cafeteria workers that they didn't have to eat broccoli because the President didn't eat it.

Young people are impressionable and once their cause has found a voice, they are nearly unstoppable in their defense of what they believe to be true. This especially holds true for those teens that rebel against their parents. They will fight tooth and nail to justify their actions. As soon as a voice of prominence arises that shares their sentiments, they smugly use it against their parents' wishes. They tout it as proof that what *they* believe, what *they* feel, what *they* want to do is their choice no matter what their parents say. After all, the President endorses it.

If a President Obama continually foists his socialistic views on America, *government good, parents bad,* our youth will have an end-all, catch-all excuse for everything from eating their vegetables to getting an abortion.

You owe it to yourself and your family to understand that such government intrusion is a planned and targeted assault on your parental rights. It is part of the liberal agenda, and it is part of Obama's agenda. Once a cycle such as this is set in motion and becomes the norm, other variations of it begin to erode other segments of society. More and more twisted laws begin to surface. People begin to lose perspective regarding human values, decency and sound, moral judgment. American government ceases to be "by the people, for the people."

I am emphatically stating that if you hold dear any moral values and the rights of all Americans to freely choose how to govern our families, you must think of the future as well as the present. You must see beyond the day-to-day issues of life and read between the lines. You have to discern the intentions of any man (or woman) who declares himself or herself fit to take the reigns of the most powerful free nation on the planet and navigate it with your family's best interests in mind.

You are an American citizen, no matter what your ethnicity. But if you are a Black American, these dynamics are even weightier, because the outcome of this historic Presidential election weighs heavily on the Black (and Hispanic) vote.

Legislating the Golden Rule

By Tiffany Owens (age 20)

Senator Barack Obama has an inclination to think the worst of people, most specifically, of my generation. His political campaign is fueled by an underlying mistrust in the American people, convinced we are helpless without the intervention of big government. Not only is he brimming with mistrust, but he also wields the equally doubtful tool of disguising it under the mask of "change."

As a member of the college generation, I find personal insult in Senator Obama's preconception that the sense of duty and service my peers and I feel towards our community and our nation is misplaced and undependable without his "promises" of government regulation.

Unfit for the Presidency

For this very reason, Senator Barack Obama is unfit for the presidency. How can a leader inspire and lead the very people in whom he lacks faith? Senator Obama has apparently confused the role of President with that of a babysitter. He arrogantly dismisses the high school and college generation as incompetent in making their own decisions and incorporating the service needs of our nation into their lifestyle.

Community service has always been a part of my high school and college experience and I assert that it is most effective when it stems from the bed of willing hearts and not the bitter seat of involuntary coercion. Bitterness towards service should be reserved exclusively for criminals as punishment. Yet, Obama insinuates that our generation should be treated the same way. His lack of confidence in my generation has driven him to attempt to create a world where we are forced to do service; instead of extending his good confidence that we will continue the legacy demonstrated by Americans of helping our fellow brother.

In essence, Sen. Obama is attempting to legislate the Golden Rule.

He fails to realize however, that in doing so he will rob the poetry from servant-hood, making it a rigid obligation. Promise of more service would do nothing more than place unwilling people on the frontlines of community service, and, despite his attempt to morph them into model citizens, would remain lacking in the heart of a servant. The value of service and the well being of the community would be utterly compromised.

Senator Obama does not trust in the good willing hearts of the American people, nor does he believe in the values of individuality or personal freedom that make this nation so great. The potential Babysitter-in-Chief is attempting to dictate how the American people can use their freedom. Citizens would be prohibited to experience their individual right to choose how to invest their freedom for the betterment of the community and their own personal gain. The pleasure of selflessness will become a mere requirement.

Willing to Serve, not Serving by Force

A brief glance into the reservoirs of community service offered in America is a blatant contradiction to Obama's claims of the necessity for government regulation. America is practically bursting at the seams with all types of community service, many of which are run by unpaid, *willing* volunteers who ask for nothing but opportunity in return. According to the Bureau of Labor and Statistics, from September 2006 to September 2007, 60.8 million Americans volunteered through or for an organization at least once.

> Senator Obama does not trust in the good willing hearts of the American people

By adding hours of community service to the tasks list of high school and college students, Obama misconstrues the true meaning of service, namely sacrifice. Good college students are busy people who multi-task and multifunction as students, employees, interns, counselors, friends, babysitters, dog-walkers, siblings, sons and daughters, and visionaries. Despite this, many of them take the time to give willingly of their abilities and resources to help their community. In return, they receive a sense of well-being that is not possible under the iron fist of legality.

Why steal their glory by forcing unwilling servants into their kingdoms of selflessness?

Not only does Obama's proposed enforced community service rob willing servants of this joy, but he also proposes to impose service hours on students whose schedules may not be able to accommodate this requirement. This regulation would compromise their effectiveness as students and the dread of obligation would dilute the potency of effective service.

Perhaps Senator Obama review closely the Thirteenth Amendment:

"Neither slavery nor involuntary servitude, except as a punishment for crime whereof the party shall have been duly convicted, shall exist within the United States, or any place subject to their jurisdiction."

Thirteenth Amendment, U.S. Constitution

The question is not whether or not voluntary service should be encouraged. The question is, "Why does Senator Obama feel it would be *his* job as President to make community service mandatory? Does Senator Obama not understand the meaning of 'no involuntary servitude'?" This would serve to be another loop for middle school, high school and college students to jump through for graduation. Not that community service should be considered a "loop" to begrudge, but that's exactly what this regulation would do.

Senator Obama is violating the true meaning of service. Making service mandatory, and issuing an incentive, is cheapening the value of service. Not only would he withhold funds from schools that could not implement service programs, he would also withhold the right of graduation to college students who may very well not be able to accommodate this regulation.

Moreover, by regulating how the citizen may serve his or her country, he is putting at dire risk the citizen's right to choose how to invest their time, freedom, and compassion. In the long run, this regulation would be the catalyst for a generation that does not understand the meaning of service. Serving our communities would become something to check off one's social bucket list issued by the government, rather than something that stems from our desire to use our freedom and our resources for the betterment of our society.

In retrospect, a fit President should be a man or woman who believes in the nobility of service when it flows from the heart; and not seek to regulate the Golden Rule or dilute the poetry of service by incentives. Most importantly, he or she would not intrude on the freedom of the people and educational systems to choose how best to implement an attitude of service within their communities. A fit President is a person who trusts the people he or she so desires to govern.

A True American
By Bethany Owens (age 18)

"What is a true American?"

A true American is not only one born in the United States of America, but one who cherishes its people, its culture, and yes, even the language. The true American holds to what America believes in, what America stands for, what America was built on. He or she embraces the freedom and equality of every man, woman, and child, and loves the country that despises racism, discrimination, and communism. American citizens hold on to what our forefathers established at the birth of our country.

Today, as true Americans, we uphold what we believe in and are determined to raise our voices against any opposition to our freedoms and liberties.

Americans stand for righteousness, truth, honesty and common sense. There is one thing that we have not forgotten that I think should concern non-Americans: we still have freedom of speech. We still have a voice, and a zeal for truth.

"A time to tear, and a time to mend, a time to be silent and a time to speak..." *Ecclesiastes 3:7*

It is time to speak up. Those who want to defend this country must do so.

Who is He? Who is She?

Many Americans don't really know what Senator Obama stands for, what he truly represents. Well, of course, Barack Obama is running for office for the presidency of the United States. I have concerns about Senator and Mrs. Obama leading this country. One of my concerns is that Mrs. Obama thinks America is a mean country. In her words:

"We're a divided country, we're a country that is "just downright mean," we are "guided by fear," we're a nation of cynics, sloth's, and complacent. "We have become a nation of struggling folks who are barely making it every day," she said, as heads bobbed in the pews. "Folks are just jammed up, and it's gotten worse over my lifetime. And, doggone it, I'm young. Forty-four!" – Michelle Obama,

2008http://gatewaypundit.blogspot.com/2008/03/michelle-obama-were-country-thats.html

Based on this statement, I'm very concerned about Mrs. Obama potentially becoming America's First Lady. Look at the quote and read it carefully. Doesn't this concern you?

There is so much to be proud of about America, but Mrs. Obama disagrees. She refers to us as "cynics, sloth's and complacent." What about all of those that fought for our freedom and allowed all of us, including Mrs. Obama to live freely in America, to attend schools and universities, and gave each citizen an opportunity for growth and prosperity? Why does she speak of America in this manner? It disturbs me. All those soldiers that gave their lives for this country (and continue to do so) did it in order to give us the freedom and the ability to fight for what we believe in.

How is it that we are "complacent" despite the fact that we were hard rugged pioneers, who worked our way to the West when we could have turned up our nose against progressing forward? Instead, we decided to push against all odds and find something better. During moments where we could have given up all hope, we fought through with our lives, kept our composure, and didn't let it get the best of us.

We succeeded but Mrs. Obama calls us "sloth's", people that sit around and wait for the world to come begging at our feet for us to get up and do something meaningful with our lives. In 1869, the Transcontinental Railroad was built to join the two coasts of the nation. Despite hardships of both nature and humanity, we triumphed; we were not slothful. These actions served to boost the economy of our nation as well to provide unprecedented opportunity for exploration and growth.

Language—According to Barack

The "embarrassment" that Senator Obama has about this country is quite lame to be honest. In his mind, Americans should speak Spanish, not English, to those who come over here from some Spanish-speaking country to make a living in America. No, we shouldn't say. "Hi" and expect them to know what to say back. Nothing against any ethnic group, being I am of mixed heritage, BUT English is our language, my friend. Americans speak English.

But…according to Mr. Obama:

"You know, it's embarrassing when Europeans come over here, they all speak English, they speak French, they speak German. And then we go over to Europe, and all we can say [is], 'Merci beaucoup.' Right? - Barack Obama, 2008

http://www.washingtontimes.com/weblogs/bellantoni/2008/Jul/08/que-obama-says-nations-kids-should-be-bilingual/

Oh excuse me, it's French. German. Whatever. Someone wants to come over to America; they should speak what we speak. This is what America is all about! This is our heritage! How can someone say we should not speak our language but others? Why should we be ashamed of ourselves for not being bilingual? I, for one, can only utter one or two words in French and I must give myself some credit—I can speak a few phrases in Spanish. I'm not downing other languages and heritages, but my goodness, embarrassed of your own country's language?

Who's Got My Back?

Remember that every citizen has a right to bear arms in self-defense and defense of his family and the state. Whether you're a man or woman of legal age, you have the individual right to possess and carry weapons in case of confrontation. This is a right of every American.

A well regulated Militia, being necessary to the security of a free State, the right of the people to keep and bear Arms, shall not be infringed.

United States Constitution, II Amendment

Now that we have that understanding, remember all of these soldiers that are fighting for our country. Think about the liberties that all these soldiers fight for. Some of you have family members, and friends, fathers and mothers in the war fight now. Now think about all that you hold dear, everything that you've fought for. Your freedom, freewill and, most of all, the feeling of being protected, is your right as an American citizen.

Don't you want to sleep with the peace that your country is well protected with the leader of the free world in the White House protecting you? Imagine that protection you have is now snatched from you and taken away. That's exactly what it will feel like if Senator Obama gets in office and decides to disarm America of our nuclear weapons.

> **Your freedom, freewill and, most of all, the feeling of being protected, is your right as an American citizen.**

Here is what he said on YouTube:

"As President, I will end misguided defense policies and stand with Caucus for Priorities in fighting special interests in Washington. First, I'll stop spending $9 billion a month in Iraq. I'm the only major candidate who opposed this war from the beginning—and as President, I will end it.

Second, I will cut tens of billions of dollars in wasteful spending. I will cut investments in unproven missile defense systems. I will not weaponize space. I will slow our development of future combat systems, and I will institute an independent defense priorities board to ensure that the Quadrennial Defense Review is not used to justify unnecessary spending.

I will not develop new nuclear weapons; I will seek a global ban on the production of fissile material, and I will negotiate with Russia to take our ICBMs off hair-trigger alert and to achieve deep cuts in our nuclear arsenals. You know where I stand."

http://www.youtube.com/watch?v=7o84PE871BE

This man is considering taking away our protection from our country! This is how he proposes to run things if he gets in office? True people of America, it is time to take a closer look at who you will be voting for.

Look inside your heart. Look at the reasons why you choose Obama. Are you sure about this step that you are taking? Are you choosing Obama because he's "Black" and it's time we have a "Black President" in the office? Think harder; think about truth, righteousness, and honesty. Think about your children, relatives and friends. Think about your life, the past, present, and future.

There is nothing more powerful then one's convictions that can turn the tables. Your freedom is yours by right; hold to your convictions and keep your freedom.

Why I Care About Education
By David Owens (age 16)

As a sixteen year old, education is very important in these years of my life. To me and a lot of other young adults across America, having quality schools is very important. Having a good environment to learn in is crucial because that environment affects the learning experience immensely.

I disagree with Mr. Obama's point of view on education, specifically because he does not support private school vouchers. To me, it would make a difference if the public schools were doing well, but they're not.

From what I have read and heard, the public school system is failing.

* Students are not faring well on national assessments. The most recent NAEP assessments indicate that less than one third of U.S. fourth graders are proficient in reading, mathematics, science, and American History.

* More than half of low income students cannot even demonstrate basic knowledge of science, reading, and history.

* U.S. eighth graders ranked 19th out of 38 countries on mathematics assessments and 18th in science.

* U.S. twelfth graders ranked 18th out of 21 countries in combined mathematics and science assessments.

Source: http://education-portal.com/articles/
Top_5_Reasons_Why_Public_Schools_Are_Failing_Our_Children.html

"According to the most recent academic comparison study by the Program for International Student Assessment, of students in 32 developed countries, 14 countries score higher than the U.S. in reading, 13 have better results in science, and 17 score above America in mathematics.

More research shows that the public school system spends more time learning in front of a television set rather than doing solid research and studying.

A survey by the Princeton Testing Service shows that American students rank highest amongst industrialized democracies for amount of time spent watching videos in class.

Source: http://www.americandaily.com/article/987

As a student, I am able to achieve a lot more in a successful school system. I do not attend private or public school, I am homeschooled; although I attended both private and public school settings in the past. I was fortunate to have attended very good and productive schools and as a result, I enjoyed my education. I am sure that most young adults in America would like to have a good experience while they are in school, and not one that causes them to frown on it.

The school vouchers would return to parents their tax dollars which they in turn could spend at a private school. Research shows that students who attend private schools rank higher in all subjects than students who attend public schools.

Mr. Obama is apparently indecisive on his position on vouchers.

In a statement on February 15, 2008, Mr. Obama said that he *would* support school vouchers because they would not hinder the education of our students.

"I will not allow my predispositions to stand in the way of making sure that our kids can learn," Mr. Obama, who has previously said he opposes vouchers, said in a meeting with the editorial board of the Milwaukee Journal-Sentinel. "We're losing several generations of kids, and something has to be done."

source: http://www.nysun.com/national/obama-open-to-private-school-vouchers/71403/

Then a few months later he changed his position:

The New York Sun on July 14, 2008, read, " Mr. Obama is saying decisively that he does not support private school vouchers, while sticking with his support for incentive pay for teachers based on their students' performance."

source: http://www.nysun.com/new-york/obama-tells-teachers-union-he-opposes-vouchers/81801/

Mr. Obama's views on school vouchers are unstable and not dependable. As far as it goes, Mr. Obama does not have the best interests for America's education system.

To conclude, Senator Obama does not agree with school vouchers, one very important part of the various issues important to America that he may not agree with. Being that education enables people to succeed, it would only be fair to assume that if Senator Obama became President, the students of this country would have poor education and other problems would rapidly arise.

I do not approve how Senator Obama is handling the education problem, and it only reflects how he will handle future problems.

CHAPTER SIX

The Protection of Human Freedom

Don't interfere with anything in the Constitution. That must be maintained, for it is the only safeguard of our liberties.

Abraham Lincoln

The Constitution is not an instrument for the government to restrain the people, it is an instrument for the people to restrain the government – lest it come to dominate our lives and interests.

Patrick Henry

Our Constitution was not written in the sands to be washed away by each wave of new judges blown in by each successive political wind.

Justice Hugo Black

The liberties of our country, the freedoms of our civil Constitution are worth defending at all hazards; it is our duty to defend them against all attacks. We have received them as a fair inheritance from our worthy ancestors. They purchased them for us with toil and danger and expense of treasure and blood. It will bring a mark of everlasting infamy on the present generation – enlightened as it is – if we should suffer them to be wrested from us by violence without a struggle, or be cheated out of them by the artifices of designing men.

Samuel Adams

The Bill of Rights is the first ten amendments to our United States Constitution.

James Madison introduced them as a series of amendments in 1789 in the First United States Congress. Ten of the amendments were ratified and became the Bill of Rights in 1791. These amendments limit the powers of the federal government and protect the rights of all citizens, residents and visitors on United States territory. Among the enumerated rights these amendments guarantee are: the freedoms of speech, press, and religion; the right to keep and bear arms; the freedom of assembly; the freedom to petition.

These Amendments play a central role in American law and government, and remain a fundamental symbol of the freedoms and culture of our great nation. One of the original fourteen copies of the Bill of Rights is on display at the National Archives in Washington, D.C.

Know Your Rights

The Bill of Rights is one of the greatest documents ever written for the protection of human freedom. It is our legacy as citizens of this great nation. When you wake up each morning, utter a silent prayer of thanks that you live in a country such as ours. Recently, I have begun to truly acquaint myself with the Bill of Rights. I confess I have not done this before, but it is now a part of our family study time. I purchased a book that breaks down our government and explains each and every aspect of it. Selena, the children and I have begun dissecting the whole design of our government and making a renewed commitment to each other to be a part of it every day for the rest of our lives.

We as Black Americans—and all other ethnicities too for that matter—need to realize what we already have as citizens of this country. If that elephant will not snap that rope tied around its ankle, and it will not go on enjoying the fruits of a fulfilling life. We all need to read and study our founding documents. When you do, you begin to fully understand what is yours by birth.

Think about it. Do you really know your rights? Are you able to assert your rights? Do you exercise these rights in a positive way? I'm not suggesting you wait until someone treats you with contempt because you are Black to exercise your rights. That's bound to happen anyway. I am talking about *living* your rights as an American in a positive way. Celebrate who you are and the freedom and opportunity you enjoy as an American, so you have no time to waste on that person who revs their engine at you or passes you up for that promotion. When you positively know your rights, you are positioned to succeed, even when you encounter others who attempt to impede your progress. This includes those closest to you.

I am not a pushover, and I am not recommending that as Black Americans we ignore injustices committed against us. I am suggesting we respond from a broader base that considers our rights as Americans, rather than simply the color of our skin. Respond from a position of principle by knowing, asserting and protecting your rights. Of course, doing so does not assure us that every outcome will be in our favor. Nor should it. It does, however, condition us to look beyond the skin. We see ourselves as free and as Americans *before* we see ourselves as Black. Doing so will broaden our outlook and the way

> **The Bill of Rights is one of the most powerful and persuasive documents you will ever read.**

we see other people. In turn, others will see us differently as well. They will see us truly for who we are—American citizens, first and foremost.

The Bill of Rights is one of the most powerful and persuasive documents you will ever read. The intense debate of brilliant men that forged these immortal words should stir the hearts of every thinking American. I say again we are blessed as Black Americans to have inherited such a document with the set of laws and individual protections that emanate from it. For the over 225 years we have existed as a nation, the words in this document have been challenged time and again, and yet we have remained steadfast in the core beliefs held in this document. We have forged on. Without a doubt, human liberty and human dignity throughout the world has benefited with every hard-won step we Americans have taken.

Grasping of the significance of our rights under our Constitution can only ensure our determination and fight to keep them. Every generation of Americans must step up and understand the precious gift we have inherited. "Precious" may not do it justice, perhaps divinely inspired comes the closest. If you ever want to appreciate America, go live in another country for even a short time. I think most of us would return and not only kiss the ground but also roll in our native soil grateful to be home. I encourage you to make the Bill of Rights required study—and even memorization—in your home; for your children's sake, if nothing else. It sings. It stirs us. It makes us want to be all we can be. It makes us feel...blessed.

Make the Bill of Rights a discussion topic at your church or school. Organize a field trip or family trip to Philadelphia and take in Independence Square or any of the great museums and monuments in Washington, DC. It will provide you with an awe-inspiring and sweeping overview of the founding of our country, all the way to the present. Black Americans are not left out of this presentation. We are there front and center where we have always been in our great march forward as a nation. You owe it to yourself and your family.

Once you truly know the Bill of Rights, you will begin to see how imperative it is that we judge a candidate for President by these standards, rather than the appearance of his skin. The Bill of Rights has absolutely nothing to do with skin color, my friends. Is Barack Obama the kind of man—with the background and solid allegiance to our Constitution—that truly grasps what this nation stands for?

I want to be absolutely sure I am not voting for a manipulative stealth candidate put in play to circumvent our Bill of Rights. We cannot, as free people, stand for further encroachments on our liberty by power hungry politicians who pander and manipulate us under the guise of being one of us and promising to take care of us.

Does the agenda of an unknown like Barack Obama introduce reforms that may fundamentally change the laws that are designed to protect us? Will they inhibit me from pursuing the simplicity of happiness without government intrusion? There are many reasons why Black Americans should have doubts about Barack Obama and any party or person who believes more government is better. Former President Ronald Reagan said it best.

Our natural, inalienable rights are now considered to be a dispensation from government, and freedom has never been so fragile, so close to slipping from our grasp as it is at this moment.

Ronald Reagan

Below I have listed the Ten Amendments from the Bill of Rights. Take time with your family and friends to read, discuss and contemplate these beautiful guarantors of your freedom. Ponder how every candidate on every level feels about these rights. Doing so will not only make you a better Black American, it will make you a better American citizen.

THE BILL OF RIGHTS

Amendment One

Congress shall make no law respecting an establishment of religion, or prohibiting the free exercise thereof; or abridging the freedom of speech, or of the press; or the right of the people peaceably to assemble, and to petition the Government for a redress of grievances.

Amendment Two

A well regulated Militia, being necessary to the security of a free State, the right of the people to keep and bear Arms, shall not be infringed.

Amendment Three

No Soldier shall, in time of peace be quartered in any house, without the consent of the Owner, nor in time of war, but in a manner to be prescribed by law.

Amendment Four

The right of the people to be secure in their persons, houses, papers, and effects, against unreasonable searches and seizures, shall not be violated, and no Warrants shall issue, but upon probable cause, supported by Oath or affirmation, and particularly describing the place to be searched, and the persons or things to be seized.

Amendment Five

No person shall be held to answer for a capital, or otherwise infamous crime, unless on a presentment or indictment of a Grand Jury, except in cases arising in the land or naval forces, or in the Militia, when in actual service in time of War or public danger; nor shall any person be subject for the same offence to be twice put in jeopardy of life or limb; nor shall be compelled in any criminal case to be a witness against himself, nor be deprived of life, liberty, or property, without due process of law; nor shall private property be taken for public use, without just compensation.

Amendment Six

In all criminal prosecutions, the accused shall enjoy the right to a speedy and public trial, by an impartial jury of the State and district wherein the crime shall have been committed, which district shall have been previously ascertained by law, and to be informed of the nature and cause of the accusation; to be confronted with the witnesses against him; to have compulsory process for obtaining witnesses in his favor, and to have the Assistance of Counsel for his defense.

Amendment Seven

In Suits at common law, where the value in controversy shall exceed twenty dollars, the right of trial by jury shall be preserved, and no fact tried by a jury, shall be otherwise re-examined in any Court of the United States, than according to the rules of the common law.

Amendment Eight

Excessive bail shall not be required, nor excessive fines imposed, nor cruel and unusual punishments inflicted.

Amendment Nine

The enumeration in the Constitution, of certain rights, shall not be construed to deny or disparage others retained by the people.

Amendment Ten

The powers not delegated to the United States by the Constitution, nor prohibited by it to the States, are reserved to the States respectively, or to the people.

CHAPTER SEVEN

The Black American Pastor
& Barack Obama

Let me start by saying that is not my intent to show disrespect to any religion. As I believe in my God, you should believe in yours. As I believe my God is the only God, so should you believe the same about your god. As I have the freedom to defend my faith, so should you have such freedom. We, as subjects of our own God, must allow the gods to settle some issues and when that time comes, we all will know who is the true and living God. Until that time, let's just keep worshipping without intruding upon each other's worship.

I was raised in the church as a little boy. It was the place where you went to enjoy fellowship with the people you knew cared about you, who would be sure you had dinner to eat, and were kept warm during the winter. I know I'm not in my senior years right now, but I remember those days when it was simple. We simply listened to the preacher talk about God's love; about living holy, and keeping order in the family.

What helped form and shape Obama's beliefs? One powerful influence was his mother. One cannot deny the influence that a mother has upon her child's beliefs.

In the Obama house [Obama's mother's], the Bible, the Koran, and the Bhagavad-Gita shared the same shelf space with books on mythology. His mother viewed them all through the eyes of the anthropologist [(the scientific study of the origin, the behavior, and the physical, social, and cultural development of humans)] she was. Religion for her was "just one of the many ways—and not necessarily the best way—that man attempted to control the unknowable and understand the deeper truths about our lives," Obama wrote in *The Audacity of Hope* published in 2006.

As Christians, our faith is not "just one of those many ways…to control the unknowable and understand the deeper truths about our lives." Faith is our way of pleasing God; and our allegiance is to God, not to faith. (Hebrews 11:6). We have an allegiance to His only Begotten Son, Jesus Christ, not to a picture of Him, or an idea about Him. Those who hold the Bible to be the infallible Word of God, by which we believe the world was made, and that all life was brought forth, have two primary calls:

Master, which is the great commandment in the law? Jesus said unto him, Thou shalt love the Lord thy God with all thy heart, and with all thy soul, and with all thy mind. This is the first and great commandment. And the second is like unto it, Thou shalt love thy neighbour as thyself.
Matthew 22:36-39

Based on Obama's own motivation for walking down the aisle to make a public confession of Christ, it appears his first reasoning was the second commandment, "*love thy neighbour as thyself*", instead of the first, "*love the Lord thy God with all thy heart, and with all thy soul, and with all thy mind.*"

By his own admission, Obama's conversion was "**a choice and not an epiphany.**" It owed less to a spiritual yearning than to recognition of the power of the Black church to change lives and society [emphasis added].

In respect to the Christian faith, it is not our choosing Christ but it is Christ choosing us.

Ye have not chosen me, but I have chosen you...   *John 15:16*

"What moved me was **the role all the congregations I worked with** played in the life of the people I was working with," [my emphasis added]

"What touched me was **how faith** [my emphasis added] bolstered them against heartache and disappointment and kept them going." Obama said in an e-mail to the Christian Science Monitor.

"Materialism alone will not fulfill the possibilities of your existence," he said. "You have to fill it with the Golden Rule. You've got to fill it with thinking about others." [emphasis added].
(Nam Y. Huh/AP/file – The Christian Science Monitor)
http://www.csmonitor.com/2007/0716/p01s01-uspo.html?page=1

It is alarmingly clear that Obama does not practice Judeo-Christianity. His own statement that he "doesn't believe that salvation is only possible through Christ" reflects this; as does his own endorsement of liberal extremists views, from gay marriage to legalized murder of full term births; which are counter to our beliefs as Christians. Regardless of Obama's ethnicity and his assumed identity as a Black American, there is yet no respecter of persons with God when it comes to the truth, nor should we as clergy compromise this truth, even if an angel appeared to us.

The apostle Paul said in Galatians it wouldn't matter if they were an angel from heaven. If they preach any other Gospel let him be accursed.

I marvel that ye are so soon removed from him that called you into the grace of Christ unto another gospel: Which is not another; but there be some that trouble you, and would pervert the gospel of Christ. But though we, or an angel from heaven, preach any other gospel unto you than that which we have preached unto you, let him be accursed. As we said before, so say I now again, If any man preach any other gospel unto you than that ye have received, let him be accursed. For do I now persuade men, or God? or do I seek to please men? for if I yet pleased men, I should not be the servant of Christ.But I certify you, brethren, that the gospel which was preached of me is not after man.   *Galatians 1:6-11*

To be fair and as balanced as possible:

- I understand that we live on this earth and that this is not heaven
- I understand that as Christians we must walk and live peaceably with all men and all faiths
- I understand that we should not insist that the President be a Christian
- I understand that Barack Obama has the right to believe what he wants to believe

The truth is *Obama is misrepresenting my faith*. The Black American community must refuse to accept his false representation of Christianity and the messages it sends to our churches. Black American clergy of all levels cannot cast aside our godly judgment to support a candidate solely because of his race. It is

> **It is a dangerous presumption to run into the voting booth and check Obama...**

a dangerous presumption to run into the voting booth and check Obama when he does not check out with our values and Christian beliefs. Obama has well-crafted plan to appeal to Black churches throughout this country, as he has done throughout his political career, and he will use any "religiously correct" coercion he can to acquire your votes and the votes of your congregation.

Had Obama not made these issues part of his politics, I would not have made it a part of my concern. However, he has and therefore, I will.

I understand that people's hearts must be changed before their actions are changed. The core objective of the Christian faith is that a person must be born again of his or her own free will. But how can they know unless the preacher can preach to them the Gospel? How will they hear the Gospel (if they choose to) if they cannot hear or be "proselyzed" (because of a law)? Then how will their hearts be transformed? Will we allow a law to neutralize the Great Commission? Further, whose command will we obey, Obama's or the Lord Jesus'?

And he said unto them, Go ye into all the world, and preach the gospel to every creature.   *Mark 16:15*

As Christians we are not first called to mankind; we are called to God. We are not empowered in and of ourselves to affect change outside His empowerment and His leading. In fact, our citizenship and allegiance is first and last to the Kingdom of God. While indeed we exercise our citizenship where we live, we do so from a higher plane of life, empowerment and expectation. Even Jesus said, "My Kingdom is not of this world..." (John 18:36).

Before the liberals jump to conclusion (of which they will anyway), as Christians, we are intimately concerned and involved with the world, and are moved by our God to serve those in the world as ambassadors of Heaven; not as a political candidate serving a party's interest or even our own. Though we see ourselves as not of this world, we have been called to be a light to the world and the salt of the earth while we are here.

Neither the light, nor the salt, originates from within man. It is not within man's ability to legislate the real change that is needed, rather regeneration from within is what brings real change. We do not attempt to elevate ourselves to God-like status by assuming we can solve every person's problem or to even act as though we don't have our own.

Jesus said:

> *For the poor always ye have with you; but me ye have not always.*
>
> *John 12:8*

As Black American pastors, it is our duty to embrace the Word of God and share it with others. It is our duty to minister to the poor, the sick and the spiritually hungry. It is also our duty and responsibility to reject and false misrepresentation of our faith, especially one that smacks in the face of our Christian beliefs. Once rejected, we must then defend it.

At the Hampton Roads Ministers Conference Barack Obama asserted that his programs should spring from "our faith, the Word, and His will." They range from a new service corps for disadvantaged youths and a program for nurses to teach low-income mothers good parenting, to more jobs programs for ex-convicts and more venture capital for minority-owned businesses. This indeed would receive applause. However, his policy is contradictory to God's word and God's will.

The following article on Obama's position for the Faith-Based Initiative is a prime example of his confusion and clear evidence of where is loyalty really lies and who his real constituents are. It is clearly not the Kingdom of God, and especially not the Black American church.

Barack Obama's pledge to embrace President Bush's Faith-Based Initiative is "hollow," Jim Towey, who headed the White House initiative from 2002 to 2006, tells Newsmax.

The reason, Towey says, is that Obama undercut his claim to support the initiative by saying he would prevent any religious group **that only hires people of the same religion** from receiving federal funds. [emphasis added]

"If you get a federal grant, **you can't use that grant money to proselytize to the people you help**, and you can't discriminate against them—or against the people you hire—on the basis of their religion," Obama said. [emphasis added]

"It's a hollow pledge to embrace President Bush's Faith-Based Initiative while abandoning one of its core principles," Towey says. "It's dead on arrival with evangelicals, **with many African-American churches,** with orthodox Jews, and I think it's a disappointment to a lot of Catholic charities out there that right now are forced to *secularize* their hiring to take federal money." [emphasis added]

"They're pressured to do this by groups like the NAACP, ACLU, and Human Rights Watch, which have made it abundantly clear they **would never, ever permit** legislation to move forward that had religious hiring protections," Towey says. [emphasis added]

Never mind that Planned Parenthood receives over $300 million a year, and they discriminate in their hiring in broad daylight, "by only hiring like-minded people," he notes. "If you're pro-life, try getting a job at Planned Parenthood. So why can't faith-based groups hire on the basis of their ideology and vision?"

Before Bush hired him, Towey was Florida's secretary of health and social services under Gov. Lawton Chiles. For 12 years, Towey was legal counsel to Mother Teresa. In 1990, he lived as a volunteer in a home she ran in Washington for people addicted to drugs or alcohol, many of whom had AIDS. In 1996, Towey founded Aging with Dignity, a Tallahassee organization that promotes better healthcare for people with terminal illness.

Obama's Faith-Based Initiative Pledge Rings Hollow Monday, July 28, 2008 By: Ronald Kessler, Newsmax.com

Many Black Americans and most Americans are also simply not aware of Obama's plan to show love to global poverty, while placing restraints on our own need to show love to the poor in our own neighborhoods.   His Global Poverty plan is going to cost taxpayers an additional $847 BILLION which we would never see, yet he does not allow us to utilize any funds for faith based programs because we would attempt to "proselytize" them.

WASHINGTON, D.C. – U.S. Senators Barack Obama (D-IL), Chuck Hagel (R-NE) and Maria Cantwell (D-WA) have introduced the Global Poverty Act (S.2433), which requires the President to develop and implement a comprehensive policy to cut extreme global poverty in half by 2015 through aid, trade, debt relief, and coordination with the international community, businesses and NGOs. Representatives Adam Smith (D-WA) and Spencer Bachus (R-AL) sponsored the House version of the bill (H.R. 1302), which passed the House in September.

Obama is adamant about making hard working Americans bankroll the worlds problems away. Take note of his comments:

"Eliminating global poverty remains one of the greatest challenges we face, with billions of people around the world forced to live on just dollars a day," said Senator Obama. "We can—and must—make it a priority of our foreign policy to commit to eliminating extreme poverty and ensuring every child has food, shelter, and clean drinking water."

"As we strive to rebuild America's standing in the world, this legislation will not only commit to reducing global poverty, but will also demonstrate our promise and support to those in the developing world. Our commitment to the global economy has to extend beyond trade agreements that are more about increasing corporate profits than about helping workers and small farmers everywhere." http://obama.senate.gov/press/071211-obama_hagel_can/

The legislation would commit the U.S. to spending 0.7 percent of gross national product on foreign aid, which amounts to a phenomenal 13-year total of $845 billion over and above what the U.S. already spends.

Obama is not only being hypocritical, he is thumbing his nose at the millions of Christ's servants who have helped those in need before faith-based initiatives was even legislated and will continue with or without its provision. Even so, how do you account for the millions upon millions of lives that have been impacted by Gospel of Jesus Christ and if Christ is in Obama's heart why wouldn't he want Christ to be in the heart of another?

John, a disciple of Christ, tells us that there are many spirits in the world that are anti-Christ or against Christ. (I'm not saying that Obama is the Anti-Christ so please don't go running to conclusions). We are simply told to "test" the spirits to know whether they are of God.

> **We are simply told to "test" the spirits to know whether they are of God.**

Beloved, believe not every spirit, but try the spirits whether they are of God: because many false prophets are gone out into the world.   1 Jo 4:1

This provides clergy and all children of God the standard by which to test truth. We are to try the spirits. What does this mean to "try" the spirits? The implication is to prove what is of God's Spirit and what is of an evil spirit or of man's own spirit.

As Christians we submit ourselves to the theocratic rule of God. We are not our own, and therefore, are not at liberty to, nor can we determine what is true in and of ourselves. Truth is not an idea. It's a person; and that person is Jesus Christ (John 14:6). We are sealed with the Holy Spirit of promise and he literally abides in us.

And I will pray the Father, and he shall give you another Comforter, that he may abide with you for ever; Even the Spirit of truth; whom the world cannot receive, because it seeth him not, neither knoweth him: but ye know him; for he dwelleth with you, and shall be in you.

John 14:14:16, 17

Jesus promised that He would send a comforter and that He [the comforter] would guide us into all truth.

Howbeit when he, the Spirit of truth, is come, he will guide you into all truth: for he shall not speak of himself; but whatsoever he shall hear, that shall he speak: and he will shew you things to come.

John 16:13

If we ignore these doctrinal positions, we will fail to safeguard our hearts and our flock. We will yield to humanisms and sound arguments that indeed tickle the ear, but are nonetheless lies. The Bible tells us, if a person brings a doctrine that is not of God, we are not to receive such one lest we be partakers of their falsehood.

If there come any unto you, and bring not this doctrine, receive him not into your house, neither bid him God speed: For he that biddeth him God speed is partaker of his evil deeds.   2 Jo
1:10,11

My objective is not to make Obama appear to be this evil person with an intentional and evil agenda. I will not judge his heart, but I will judge his doctrine as it pertains to the Christian standard. Obama is not a Christian and does not share the values of Christianity. I will merely use his own words to *judge his position* towards the Christian faith.

"We must talk and reach for common understandings," Obama said, "precisely because all of us are imperfect and **can never act with the certainty that God is on our side.**" [Emphasis added]

"I came to realize that **without a vessel for my beliefs, without an unequivocal commitment** to a particular community of faith, I would be consigned at some level to remain apart, free in the way my mother was free, but also alone in the same way she was ultimately alone." [Emphasis added]

These statements are directly opposed to one another. To first imply that we can never act with the certainty that God is on our side is simply absurd and accuses God of being unfaithful to His children! And then you die? To be absent from the body is to be present with the Lord (2 Cor. 5:8), and this is our hope that we shall forever reign with Him.

I am with you alway, even unto the end of the world. Amen.

Mat 28:20

... I will not leave you comfortless: I will come to you.

John 14:18

... for he hath said, I will never leave thee, nor forsake thee.

Hebrews 13:5

If we cannot be certain that God is on our side, how can there be a basis of "unequivocal commitment to a particular community of faith"? This is precisely my point. Obama does not have a commitment to a particular community of faith, and therefore to a specific

CONCLUSION

If we, as Americans, both Black and White, respond as true citizens of this great country and allow the facts and the spirit of the issues speak forth, the obvious becomes profoundly clear as it pertains to FREEDOM: Barack Obama is not right for America.

Whether or not we accept these facts will be determined by our capacity to set aside preconceptions and mindsets that have done more to hinder us than the act of racism itself. Without a doubt, you will have unfairness in every sector of society. By no means does my position deny these acts are in existence. Such is life. Nor is it my intention to condone or dismiss them. I choose instead to join those who are diligently building relationships that are thriving toward horizons that provide a positive future for my country.

Black or White, we must agree Obama's mindset, spirit and policies do not share this hope. His idea of change is to shackle our freedoms; expand the nanny state, create deep divides among all facets of society, and cater to unorthodox ideals contrary to those on which this nation was built. We will be faced with the 'isms' of SOCIALISM and COMMUNISM that would make racism seem like child's play. I am certain none of us want this, no matter what our color, creed or religion.

Now is not a time to hide behind indifference. It is a time for us to stand as one in accord for life, liberty and the pursuit of happiness, the basic necessities for a healthy democracy. As American citizens, we are obligated to protect these fundamental rights. Let us join together, not as a race of color, but as a race of FREE people. Let us continue to press toward solutions within our homes, churches and communities. Let us even continue to disagree. The reality of freedom gives us the right to do so. When we no longer disagree, we have allowed the Obamas of this world to make it politically incorrect or potentially illegal to believe and live the way we choose.

We must all rise upon this common platform and declare:

WE ARE PROUD TO BE AMERICANS OF EVERY COLOR IN
THE LAND OF THE FREE, HOME OF THE BRAVE!

Conclusion

iTouch Publishers
www.itouchpublishers.com
P.O. Box 1395 • Fuquay-Varina, NC 27526
800-791-5806

COMING FALL 2008 / SPRING 2009

THE WINNING FAMILY
By The Owens Family

The Winning Family is not just a cliché to us. We are living what you are about to read everyday. It's not over-rated philosophical gibberish that you'll need to have a degree philosophy to decode. Nor is it designed to be easy. You'll have to apply the simple truths you're about to experience with courage, tenacity, and a lot of prayer. If you do, you'll experience the immediate consequence of applying these winning principles that we have learned over the years as a family. *Expected Release Date : Spring 2009*

KEEP THE VISION ALIVE: MAKE,
DON'T BREAK, THE MAN OF VISION
By Selena Owens

When God has placed a visionary in your life, there are experiences that will make you or break you. Mrs. Owens is very familiar with working with a visionary and in this book, she brings to the forefront the call of wives to empower their husbands in fulfilling the vision. *Topics include: Characteristics of a Man of Vision, Understanding the Vision, Selfishness, Pride, Prayer, Support, A Time to Sow. Workbook included inside of book.*

Expected Release Date: Spring 2009

Persuasions

Coming
Fall 2008

PERSUASIONS
By Tiffany Owens

Persuasions are a powerful force of ideas that threaten our freedom as individuals. Founded on fear and a tainted view of God, these persuasions taint our identity and our understanding of love, life, and truth, and they are a force that remains unchallenged for our generation. Written with honesty and wit, Persuasions is an exposure of these influences, and a celebration of the most powerful persuasion of all: the persuasion of God's love. www.persuasions.us
Expected Release Date: Fall 2008